Reviewers on Gabriel Zaid's *So Many Books*

"Zaid traces the preoccupation with reading back through Dr. Johnson, Seneca, and even the Bible ('Of making many books there is no end'). He emerges as a playful celebrant of literary proliferation."
— *The New Yorker*

"An appealing, meditative collection of thoughts and observations on the book industry and the state of literature in the early 21st century."
— *Publishers Weekly*

"Zaid's crisp reasoning, matched by Wimmer's elegant translation, makes *So Many Books* indispensable reading for agents, publishers and booksellers. At a time when we risk being drowned in a flood of print, it is a timely reminder that 'the measure of our reading should...be not the number of the books we've read, but the state in which they leave us.'"
— *Financial Times*

"Gabriel Zaid takes a provocative approach to books, reading, and publishing...*So Many Books* is bound to inspire discussion among those who write, publish, read, and sell books."
— *Bloomsbury Review*

"This small book is a gem: an absorbing conversation about the whole point of reading, the surplus of titles. and our own lack of time."
— Alasdai

"*So Many Books* is a whole
— *T0273357*

PAUL DRY BOOKS

Philadelphia 2008

THE SECRET OF FAME

The Literary Encounter
in an Age of Distraction

by GABRIEL ZAID

Translated by Natasha Wimmer

First Paul Dry Books Edition, 2008

Paul Dry Books, Inc.
Philadelphia, Pennsylvania
www.pauldrybooks.com

Text type: Cochin
Display type: Zapf Renaissance Book

1 3 5 7 9 8 6 4
Printed in the United States of America

Library of Congress Cataloging-in-Publication Data

Zaid, Gabriel.
    The secret of fame / Gabriel Zaid ; translated by Natasha Wimmer
        p.   cm.
    Includes bibliographical references.
    ISBN 978-1-58988-038-2 (alk. paper)
    I. Title.
    PQ7298.36.A5S43 2008
    864'.64—dc22

                                                    2008001387

Contents

THE SECRET
OF FAME

CHAPTER 1

Catching Miracles

THERE ARE PHRASES that call attention to themselves, that distract from the matter at hand and surprise even those who utter them. It's as if they've appeared out of thin air, like a miracle or a sudden revelation; as if they had readers before they had an author. It's there, in that moment of recognition, that the origin of literature lies. Phrases that are noticed, admired, and repeated become texts and begin to circulate, unattributed and unregulated. The author is lost from sight.

Today we've arrived at the opposite extreme. The author attracts attention even as the work is lost from sight. People would rather talk about writers than read what they've written. The spotlight is on TV interviews, celebrities, photographs, anecdotes, prizes, advances, and sales rather than on sentences, images, scenes, characters, or ideas that linger in the memory.

The first "texts" committed to memory—sayings, songs—were short, oral, and anonymous, possibly preceding cave painting. The first literary writings — short and anonymous — appeared in Mesopotamia and Egypt four or five thousand years ago; they were spells, ritual chants, and invocations engraved on tombs. Three or four thousand years ago, again in Mesopotamia, the first long texts — *Gilgamesh, Enuma Elish* — were composed, still anonymous and oral. By the eighth century B.C., in Palestine, the prophet Amos was writing like an author addressing himself to the public, and by the seventh century B.C., in Greece, Hesiod was doing the same. Both Amos and Hesiod left some reference to themselves in their texts, which were no longer short, oral, or anonymous. One thousand years later, at the end of the fourth century, the autobiographical poems of Gregory of Nazianzus and the *Confessions* of St. Augustine took their authors as primary subject. In the eighteenth century, the very lives of Voltaire, Franklin, Johnson, Rousseau, and Goethe seem projects undertaken in order to create a persona. Today, the author as work, as larger-than-life character created for the purposes of myth and the market, is a common phenomenon.

Fame also dates back to prehistoric times. Poems about legendary characters composed by unknown authors grew famous. Then the writers themselves became legendary. The long evolution of fame stretches from anonymous creation to a leading role for the author, from the spoken word to writing, from microtext to complete works.

Fame concentrates society's attention on a few names. This can be a good thing. It keeps us reading the great books, keeps us revisiting the great works of art. But fame can also be a bad thing. It keeps us focused on names, not on the living experience of great works.

Great works focus our minds, speak to the best in us, and spark our imagination. We feel more alive, more engaged in meaningful conversation with life. Reality makes more sense. We make more sense. It's as if we've experienced a miracle, as if we've been granted access to eternity. It's only natural to spread the word, to share the experience, to bring that higher level of living to ordinary life. As great writing leads to great writing, conversation about great works may itself become great—or it may just be noise about big names.

Fame (i.e., being talked about) can also seem like a passport to eternity, to an existence on a higher level, outside ordinary life. The sculptor becomes a sculpture created by others, a monument, an object of admiration and even idolatry, set upon a pedestal and excluded from ordinary give and take. Rilke said that Rodin was solitary before he became famous, and more solitary after he became famous, because fame is the accumulation of misunderstandings around new names.

Nowadays experts sell secrets for the creation of useful misunderstandings and sculpt the would-be famous for the limelight. But there are no experts in the art of catching miracles. Authors fortunate enough to have caught—by chance, craft, or inspiration—a miracle in their writing should not complain too much. They got the better part, after all.

CHAPTER 2
Quotations and Aphorisms

FRAGMENTS QUOTED BY OTHERS are all that remain of many of the books of antiquity. Isolated phrases, sometimes apocryphal, are all that circulate of many books that still exist in their entirety.

Not just any fragment becomes detached and takes on a life of its own. The physical fragmentation of the Dead Sea Scrolls may isolate a phrase that will never catch on: "and then they return from the water" (4Q414 F.12), for example, interesting only in the reconstruction of baptismal rites. In order for a fragment to circulate, it must be a memorable text, interesting in and of itself though it's part of a larger work. It must be suited to being passed from mouth to mouth; it must be resonant. Or it must be made resonant through the creative lapses of memory that improve, distort, or invent, as is often the case with sayings and popular songs, tumbled along by tradition like stones in a river.

Even when they come from written literature, fragments quoted from memory circulate as if they were oral literature. Texts are transformed, variations appear, the words of one author are attributed to another, or the author is lost in anonymity. Significantly, when these fragments return to the world of books in collections of phrases, they are almost never properly documented as quotations verifiable by comparison with the original. They are collected (sometimes they just pile up) with a simple nod to the presumed author. They are treated like folkloric materials which change like faces with the passage of time, the originals forgotten.

No one reads Jean-Baptiste Say anymore, but his famous law—which he never wrote, though it's a good summary of his position on the subject —is quoted: "Supply creates its own demand" (Thomas Sowell, *Say's Law: An Historical Analysis*). Few have read Lord Acton, but many quote his "Power corrupts," although the phrase (from a letter by the author, never published in his lifetime) is: "Power tends to corrupt and absolute power corrupts absolutely" (Lord Acton, *Essays on Freedom and Power*, ed. Gertrude Himmelfarb). Similarly (even in respectable collections), there are two or three different versions of George Santayana's "Those who cannot remember the past are condemned to repeat it," although it comes from a book (*The Life of Reason*, abridged, vol. I, chap. 10). Just as a translation can improve the original (in "About William Beckford's *Vathek*," from *Other Inquisitions*, Borges jokes that "The original is unfaithful to the translation"), the original versions of many famous phrases can be disappointing when compared to the remembered version.

The appeal of quoted fragments can be so great that it relegates an author's entire oeuvre to the shadows (as with Acton and Say). Or it may simply reduce that oeuvre to a mounting of glittering phrases. Calderón de la Barca's *Life Is a Dream* seems contained in the climactic moment of reading or hearing the last lines of the second act: "for life is a dream, and dreams are only dreams." Orson Welles mocked those who went to see Shakespeare's plays to recognize the famous lines. There's even an epigram on the subject by Henry C. Bunner: "Shakespeare was a dramatist of note who lived by writing things to quote" (Evan Esar, *The Dictionary of Humorous Quotations*).

Perhaps as a result, writers with literary ambition have been emboldened to assert their creative freedom by ignoring the mounting and setting straight out to write the gems, without waiting for posterity. Perhaps the first to speak of fragmentary texts as characteristic of modernity was Friedrich Schlegel: "Many works of the ancients have become fragments. Many works of the moderns are fragments from birth." This fragment appeared (unattributed) in the literary almanac *Athenaeum* (1798) that Schlegel published with his brother August, both devoted scholars of the classics, like all the German Romantics (Friedrich Schlegel, *Fragments*).

Almanacs were the first periodical publications in the West. They appeared in the twelfth century, transforming the astronomical compendiums of the Arabs into liturgical annuals. With the printing press, they became bestsellers, offering agricultural and nautical information along with bits of practical advice. (In the same tradition, the *Calendario del más antiguo Galván* has been published in Mexico since 1826.) The insertion of microtexts was prompted by a problem with layout that magazines still face today. Each section and article looks best if it begins at the head of a page, but nothing guarantees that it will be the right length to conclude at the foot of a page. There may be blank spaces at the end, to be filled with vignettes or short texts. For the reader, this microtextual filler (sayings, advice, anecdotes) was very appealing. Benjamin Franklin made a living as the printer, editor, and author of *Poor Richard's Almanack* (1732–57) with sayings of his own (or reworkings of other people's sayings) that are still in circulation today. (Curiously, Georg Christoph Lichtenberg never published his famous aphorisms, despite editing the Göttingen almanac, the

Göttinger Taschenkalender, 1776–98.) The Schlegel brothers' almanac (1798–1800) was already practically a literary magazine, inspired by Schiller's and Goethe's *Horen* (1795–97) and *Musenalmanach* (1796–1800). It published hundreds of anonymous fragments by Friedrich and August Schlegel, Schleiermacher, Novalis, and others.

Schlegel's observation was something of a banner for the Romantic movement. But the practice of the intentional fragment already existed. Pascal wrote fragmentarily toward an apologia of Christian faith, which he left half-finished and which is now known as the *Pensées:* "I shall here write my thoughts without order, and not perhaps in unintentional confusion; that is true order, which will always indicate my object by its very disorder" (373, trans. W. F. Trotter). But the model that proved decisive for modern letters had appeared a few years before. *Reflections; or Sentences and Moral Maxims* (1665) by La Rochefoucauld polished the maxim like a literary jewel. It even went so far as to (implicitly) introduce games between author and reader, in the space of a few words. One of these games (still imitated today) is to feign a move in one direction and then surprise the reader by ending up somewhere else, for example: "We all have strength enough to bear the misfortunes of others" (*Maxims* XIX, trans. Howard E. Hugo). The literary salons fed this sharp sense of play (orally) and fed on it (literarily) as it was developed by the French moralists La Rochefoucauld, La Bruyère, Vauvenargues, Chamfort, and Joubert.

And yet, the deliberate creation of fragmentary texts is not a modern phenomenon. These texts appeared in prehistoric times, although few are aware of it because our attention is focused on the classics (the great books read through the ages) as source, not on the sources of the classics (the memorable, anonymous, oral scraps that are still being created). Our ignorance of this reality (prehistoric and current) skews our perspective and distorts the facts, making it seem as if microtexts are fragments detached from larger texts, not works in and of themselves.

Ernst Robert Curtius (*European Literature and the Latin Middle Ages*) discusses the collections of classical maxims assembled by medieval scholars for the purposes of memorization, consultation, and quotation. In the garden of the classics, a collector would select, clip, and arrange memorable phrases in a literary bouquet, or anthology. As it happens, Curtius's analyses perform a similar task: he himself uncovers a question that hadn't been systematically explored, tracing it from the Greeks to Goethe, and compiling the quotations that confirm the question's existence and evolution. It's an impressive method, but it assumes that clichés, stylistic traits, figures of speech, motifs, symbols, metaphors, and examples are passed on from one work to another just as genes are transferred from living bodies to their descendants, without ever being bodies themselves. So it is in many cases, but we mustn't forget the independent microtexts, those small works of art, that were passed from mouth to mouth before being incorporated into larger Greek, Latin, medieval, and European works.

Aristotle incorporates a thought that had an author (although no one knows who the author was) into his *Nicomachean Ethics*, a thought that still circulates in many languages, transformed in the ways one might expect (different bird, different season): "For one swallow does not make a summer, nor does one day; and so too one day, or a short time, does not make a man blessed and happy" (*The Complete Works*, revised Oxford translation, *Nicomachean Ethics*, book I, 1098a). Thanks to this kind of borrowing, oral literature is haphazardly preserved in writing. The *Iliad* and the *Odyssey* circulated orally centuries before they began to circulate in writing in the sixth century B.C. (canonical already), and the first critical editions appeared in the second century B.C. But to this day no one has bothered to collect the jokes that circle the planet, to document them scientifically, to build databases and edit critical editions. It doesn't seem a literary project worthy of a doctorate.

A similar project would be to gather all the lullabies (lyrics and music) sung by all the tribes on the planet. Unfortunately, indigenous languages (which continue to disappear) have been of more interest to linguists than to anthologists. The transcription of oral literature doesn't seem to merit the same rigor as the transcription of written work, textual criticism, interpretation. In Mexico, for example, the great studies of indigenous literature are based on transcriptions made centuries ago by missionaries. Almost no one bothers to make new transcriptions, not even writers today who set out to write poems and stories in those indigenous languages.

Oral literature didn't disappear with writing, nor will it disappear. It circulates blithely, anonymous and unregulated. It passes from one group to another, one country to another, one language to another, traveling from mouth to mouth, though also spread by other means (written, audiovisual, electronic). No distinction is made between thousand-year-old creations, week-old creations, or instant creations by someone who happens to be talking just now (maybe aware that what he's saying has never been said before, or maybe not; maybe reinventing it without realizing that the same thing was said in another time or another country; maybe knowingly adapting it for the circumstances; maybe remembering or thinking he remembers the author, or making up a name).

According to Karl Popper (*The World of Parmenides*), the pre-Socratics invented the critical tradition. Instead of repeating traditional beliefs, they questioned them and, at the same time, questioned one another. With the pre-Socratics, the historic novelty of quoting is born, thanks to which fragments of lost works are preserved, or notice is at least given of their existence. Heraclitus: "Learning of many things does not teach intelligence; if so it would have taught Hesiod and Pythagoras, and again Xenophanes and Hecataeus." But fortunately longer texts by Hesiod still exist, while only fragments or quotations remain of the work of so many authors. These quotations, paraphrases, and summaries aren't just incomplete. They may also be scarcely representative, playing up aspects that interest the author who cites them, rather than the author cited. (For example, according to Curtius, Ovid's medieval compilers chose only those phrases that seemed edifying.) And memory isn't just selective. It also tends to smooth over rough edges. Were all of Heraclitus's maxims really so pithy? "You would not step twice into the same river." "The path up and down is one and the same." "If one does not expect the unexpected one will not find it out..." "I searched out myself."

G. S. Kirk and J. E. Raven (*The Presocratic Philosophers*) think the answer is yes, that Heraclitus's maxims were "for the most part obviously framed as oral apophthegms rather than as parts of a discursive treatise." Eric A. Havelock (*The Liberal Temper in Greek Politics*) says the same thing about fragments from Democritus: "The rounded sentence began its career in the preliterate days of oral communication, when indoctrination depended on word of mouth and retention of doctrine depended on the memory. Democritus himself was a writer, but he wrote in a period when readers were still outnumbered by listeners. It is therefore not surprising that he compressed his ideas into gnomic formulations, for he can be pictured, like the poets who were his contemporaries, as composing under what we may call a form of audience-control. Collections of *gnomae*, therefore, stamped with the hallmark of individual thinkers were characteristic of the first stage of Greek prose writing. But the anthologies of such which were accumulated systematically in the Hellenistic Age and later, and which dominated so much thinking and writing in later antiquity and the Middle Ages, were devoted to the special task of preserving in an epoch of books and readers that kind of material which was still suitable for oral memorization."

The fragment as independent work isn't a feature of modern times, but of prehistoric times. The first microtexts weren't the jottings of the Romantics, "fragments from birth," or the maxims of La Rochefoucauld, or even the aphorisms of Heraclitus and Democritus; they were popular sayings that predated writing. The creation of memorable microtexts didn't stop with the appearance of writing. It continued in the traditional fashion and also in written form, thanks to a great critical thinker and original writer: Heraclitus. According to Havelock (*The Literate Revolution in Greece and Its Cultural Consequences*), the authors of philosophical poems (Parmenides, Xenophon, Empedocles) disputed the thinking of Homer and Hesiod, but they still wrote in Homeric hexameter. Heraclitus wrote in prose instead, moving away from the hexameter and recitation with musical accompaniment, turning instead to the aphoristic phrasing of the traditional adage and transforming it with clear stylistic intent.

Many things tumble together in the river of tradition: oral microtexts from millennia ago and from today; written microtexts (original, revised, or transcribed) by known, unknown, or improperly attributed authors; the remnants of long (or short) texts, in the form of fragments, quotations, or references; compilations of selected phrases;

professional aphorisms (Hippocratic, legal, political, and even engineering); literary gems (from La Rochefoucauld to Cioran); modern fragmentary prose. The back and forth between the heard and the read, the original and the quoted, the anonymous and the attributed, the old and the new, the short and the long, makes literary reconstruction difficult, blurs everything.

A significant loss on this turbulent river is historical and genealogical perspective. Just as ahistorical criteria prevail in the study of folklore (regional, functional, or thematic distinctions are easier to draw), attribution and therefore chronologies are frequently false or dubious in the study of quotations and aphorisms (never mind sayings). In *They Never Said It: A Book of Fake Quotes, Misquotes, and Misleading Attributions*, Paul F. Boller Jr. and John George identify more than 200 apocryphal quotes. Robert K. Merton devoted years and a whole book (*On the Shoulders of Giants*) to the study of a single statement by Newton, which became famous: "If I have seen further it is by standing on the shoulders of Giants." It turned out that it wasn't Isaac Newton (1643–1727) who coined it, or George Herbert (1593–1633) or Robert Burton (1577–1640) or Diego de Estella (1524–78), but Bernard of Chartres (12th cent.), as his disciple John of Salisbury wrote in the year 1159 (*Metalogicon*, book III, chap. 4).

On the basis of seemingly insignificant fragments, paleontologists reconstruct the possible evolution of the species. On the basis of the geographic distribution of languages and genes, Luigi Luca Cavalli-Sforza (*Genes, Peoples, and Languages*) has established great genealogies of the migration of peoples and the evolution of languages. In turn, epidemiologists, working from databases that reach all the way down to the level of each infected person, are able to reconstruct the genealogy of an epidemic. It's perfectly possible to apply similar methods to the genealogy of all kinds of sayings, quotations, and aphorisms. The creation that seems anonymous today, or is improperly attributed, might then take on a personal face and be set in historical context as well as comparative and evolutionary perspective.

CHAPTER 3
Exotic Quotations

BOOKS AND ARTICLES published in New York (or Paris) mostly quote books and articles published in New York (or Paris). In some sense, it's natural for metropolises to be provincial: the development of a creative conversation and the excitement that makes it lively has at its center a local debate. Conversely, it's a clear sign of underdevelopment when publications don't cite local authors so as *not* to seem provincial. Theirs is the haughtiness of Groucho Marx: "I don't care to belong to any club that will have me as member." In underdeveloped countries, the important conversations are those that are followed from a distance, like a performance. To be on the periphery consists precisely in not being centered in oneself, in believing that real life is elsewhere.

Julio Ramón Ribeyro complained in *Prosas apátridas:* "A Latin American writer quotes forty-five authors in an eight-page article. Here are some of them: Homer, Plato, Socrates, Aristotle,

Heraclitus, Pascal, Voltaire, William Blake, John Donne, Shakespeare, Bach, Chekhov, Tolstoy, Kierkegaard, Kafka, Marx, Engels, Freud, Jung, Husserl, Einstein, Nietzsche, Hegel, Cervantes, Malraux, Camus, etc." Wilfrido H. Corral ("El desmenuzamiento de la autoridad de la cita y lo citado") takes Ribeyro's remark as epigraph, softening it by stating that the same obsession exists in all literatures, and making an important point: "It's only recently that Latin Americans have begun to cite Latin Americans."

It must also be said that the quotable canon varies from time to time and place to place. Ribeyro's list is dated: it was composed around 1960, before Foucault, Althusser, and academic Marxism. And to Corral's observation one might add that the recent phenomenon has come about since the boom in Latin American novels published in Barcelona, Paris, and New York around 1970, although Latin Americans were already quoting one another during the first boom (in poetry, at the beginning of the twentieth century).

Meanwhile, Latin American academics (who've never had a boom) religiously quote the most obscure European and American professors, ignoring their Latin American colleagues, not to mention non-academic writers. References to the work of the foreign institutions where they received their doctorates are a way of reminding others where they studied and of cloaking themselves in the authority of those institutions. They cite, translate, and extend invitations to their foreign professors, apply their methods, and dream about being authorized as their representatives, in charge of research outposts. Their greatest ambition is to publish where their professors have published. All of this is respectable, but not the same as striking up a local conversation. The miracle that created Socrates, Plato, and Aristotle was sparked in a different way: by raising the level of the local discourse.

And yet, it must be acknowledged how difficult and even impossible it can be to raise the level of conversation in a community numbed by the struggle for survival or the obsession with prosperity. Even in vigorous societies (it mustn't be forgotten that Sparta was as powerful as Athens), the conditions may be unfavorable for creative freedom. Would it have been better if Rubén Darío had stayed in Metapa, Joseph Conrad in Berdichev, Ezra Pound in Hailey, or T. S. Eliot in St. Louis? Pound went so far as to say that it was impossible to write important poetry in the United States: it was necessary to leave the country. Eliot went to the extreme of becoming a British subject. Conrad went even further: he gave up his native language.

A first version of *The Waste Land* had as epigraph Kurtz's final judgment of his "civilizing" life in the Belgian Congo ("The horror! The horror!", *Heart of Darkness*). About this epigraph, Pound wrote to Eliot: "I doubt if Conrad is weighty enough to stand the citation" (*The Waste Land. A Facsimile and Transcript of the Original Drafts Including the Annotations of Ezra Pound*). The final version is equipped with an epigraph weighty enough for anyone: "I saw with my own eyes the Sybil at Cumae dangling in a bottle, and when the children asked her: 'What do you want, Sybil?' she used to answer: 'I want to die'" (trans. J. P. Sullivan, slightly altered). The dialogue was quoted in Greek, the rest in Latin. Not only that: although *The Waste Land* was published with scholarly notes (unusual for a poem), the author of the epigraph is not credited, nor is the source text cited. Eliot elegantly assumes that he belongs to a club where everyone reads Latin and Greek and will immediately recognize passage 48 from book XV (*Cena Trimalchionis*) of Petronius's *Satyricon,* which describes the lavish and ridiculous dinner hosted by a nouveau riche. Thus, in sibylline fashion, Eliot compares the "civilizing" London of the British Empire with Nero's Rome, and satirizes himself and Pound as *métèques.* One can't ask more of an exotic quote, lavishly served up by a nouveau British citizen.

The exotic quotations of the periphery-dwellers (provincials or *métèques*) must be distinguished from the exotic quotations of the residents of the metropolis. When Michel Foucault quotes Jorge Luis Borges, or Jürgen Habermas quotes Octavio Paz, they aren't boasting of a familiarity with the classics. They're boasting of being brave Marco Polos who've journeyed to the ends of the earth and come back laden with treasure. Quoting the classics is nothing compared to quoting books or documents unknown even to specialists: books by exotic authors, from remote cultures, or in obscure languages. Miguel de Unamuno says somewhere that he was fascinated by the big illustrated volumes of *México a través de los siglos [Mexico Through the Centuries]* that his father brought from Tepic, where he was a baker, and that he even dreamed about learning Nahuatl: "Then you could really put on airs. Everybody knows Greek. But Nahuatl?" (I quote from memory).

Alfonso Reyes published a volume of *Burlas literarias [Literary Lampoons] 1919–1922*, written with Enrique Díez-Canedo, to mock the snobbery of exotic quotations. For example: the alleged discovery of a medieval "Debate of Wine vs. Beer," in which the footnote to line 119 explains the word "footballer" by making reference to Gilbert Murray, *Greek Sport in the Vth Century and After: Foot Ball, etc.*, Oxford, 1923.

Jorge Luis Borges takes the game further, and not only publishes fake exotic quotes but intercalates them with real quotes that seem fake, as in "The Analytic Language of John Wilkins" (*Other Inquisitions*). Wilkins really did exist, and in 1668 he really did publish *An Essay Towards a Real Character and a Philosophical Language,* whose "600 pages in quarto" propose a world language based on a classification of everything in the universe. In the middle of a series of arguments intended to demonstrate that "it is clear that there is no classification of the Universe that is not arbitrary and full of conjectures," Borges suddenly quotes (without quotation marks, page references, or bibliographic data) a classification so exotic it can only be of his own invention. According to "a certain Chinese encyclopedia entitled *The Celestial Emporium of Benevolent Knowledge,*" "animals can be divided into (a) those belonging to the Emperor, (b) those that are embalmed, (c) those that are tame, (d) pigs, (e) sirens, (f) imaginary animals, (g) wild dogs, (h) those included in this classification, (i) those that are crazy-acting, (j) those that are uncountable, (k) those painted with the finest brush made of camel hair, (l) miscellaneous, (m) those which have just broken a vase, and (n) those which, from a distance, look like flies" (trans. Will Fitzgerald).

To cite this elaborate literary game by an obscure writer of the antipodes was truly exotic in

Paris, and it was even more exotic to write in the preface of *The Order of Things* (1966): "This book first arose out of a passage in Borges, out of the laughter that shattered, as I read the passage, all the familiar landmarks of my thought..." Fortunately for the many readers who discovered Borges through Foucault, *The Order of Things* became a worldwide academic bestseller. Quoting Borges stopped being exotic. It became part of the local conversation in the metropolises. That's why daring Latin Americans now feel authorized to quote him as a classic, in any piece less than eight pages long that cites more than forty-five authors, like this one.

CHAPTER 4

Misused Quotations

ALL QUOTED TEXT, by definition, is out of context.
It appears in the course of a second discourse that
isn't the original. Transcribed or recorded from
memory, literal or altered, intentionally or not, it
acquires a slightly or a completely different meaning, even if it's an exact quote. In this sense, it's the
work of a second author, like translations or musical arrangements.

One of many possible examples: In English, the
phrase "Who watches the watchmen?" is used in
political spheres to express the concern that those
in power will exercise a control not subject to control. But it comes from a misogynistic poem by
Juvenal (*Satire* VI, trans. Rolfe Humphries):

> But the question arises,
> *Who will be guarding the guards?* They know
>   enough to be silent,
> They get paid in kind, and your wife has the
>   cunning to know this,

Making her first misplays with the spies you have
    ordered to watch her.

This political use of an apolitical phrase is an
example of the shifts in meaning that a quoted,
referenced, imitated, parodied, or plagiarized text
undergoes. These shifts (brilliant or pedestrian,
legitimate or spurious) are the work of a second
author, even if no one knows who he or she is. The
transformation may be anonymous and even acci-
dental, but not knowing who coined a particular
reading of a phrase by Juvenal doesn't mean the
process isn't creative. The new meaning is and
isn't contained in the original poem.

Misused quotations are most frequently condemned for distorting the original author's intent,
crediting him for something that was really created by the second author. The examples are infinite. Paul F. Boller Jr. devotes an entire book to
the gathering and cataloging of misused quotations in the mid-twentieth century American press
in *Quotemanship: The Use and Abuse of Quotations for
Polemical and Other Purposes*. But there are many
other forms of misuse.

Quoting to hide an absence of thought is a
smug way of remaining silent, criticized since
antiquity. Socrates reproaches Protagoras for it
(*Protagoras*): Don't quote Simonides to me, because we'll be like men incapable of speech, men

who only listen to the music they hire to make their gatherings pleasant. What do you think? Don't you have anything to say?

Seneca writes something like this to the disciple who asks him for philosophers' maxims to memorize (*Letters to Lucilius*, XXXIII): You don't need them. It's time for you to make memorable remarks yourself.

Those who quote the classics to flatter themselves have also been criticized (as the reader of the previous quotes might suspect). Cervantes, in the prologue to *Don Quixote*, apologizes for publishing it "without notes in the margins or annotations at the end of the book," "full of citations from Aristotle, Plato, and the entire horde of philosophers," so that "readers are moved to admiration and consider the authors to be well-read, erudite, and eloquent men"; because "I am by nature too lazy and slothful to go looking for authors to say what I know how to say without them" (trans. Edith Grossman).

Distorting, dissembling, and boasting also lead to the opposite form of abuse: not citing the author, or helping oneself to ideas, themes, approaches, devices, insights, and even the exact words without acknowledging it. Aristophanes, in *The Clouds* (553), accuses Eupolis of having plagiarized one of his comedies: *Maricas* "was a rehash of my *Knights*." Martial (*Epigrams*) mocks a poet who has plagiarized him without changing a thing except his speaking style: "The verses you are reciting, Fidentinus, are mine: but recited so badly that they begin to sound like yours."

Appropriation without acknowledgment may sometimes be a refinement required by good academic manners. Above, for example, if I hadn't included the number 553, it would have looked as if I were quoting in the classical manner, from memory; by including it, it looks as if I have a Greek or bilingual edition at hand, or at least an edition with numbered lines. Actually, I found the accusation of plagiarism and the exact reference in the *Oxford Classical Dictionary* under "Plagiarism." And the edition I cite is the paperback edition of *The Complete Plays* translated by Paul Roche. But none of this (the information taken from dictionaries, popular editions, works from outside the world of academia) should be cited, even if used. It isn't elegant.

In 1673, Jacob Thomasius cataloged various elegant forms of misuse: giving a misleading title to a collection of texts by different authors in order to make it sound like a book of one's own, not a collection; stealing an idea and not citing the author; citing the author, but on a minor point rather than the critical one, to cover up the main theft; presenting what was stolen in a "higher" context, thereby using the quote but giving it a negative spin and criticizing its limitations, which are revealed to be serious; or boldly accusing the first author of plagiarism in order to get the jump on his possible accusation and discredit him from the start (*Dissertatio philosophica de plagio literario*, quoted by Anthony Grafton, *The Footnote**: *A Curious History*). He might also have included the saying "Perish those who said it before us" (*Pereant qui ante nos nostra dixerunt*), collected by Saint Jerome (*Commentary on Ecclesiastes*).

Grafton, a history professor himself, describes in his first chapter how historians use citations to accredit themselves and discredit others. For example: by making spiteful mentions, which may be reduced to a simple cf. (confer, compare to what so-and-so says). Instead of presenting and debating a counterargument, which is to lend it importance, one can simply say: This is the truth, although others may not have grasped it. Cf. so-and-so.

If more is needed, there follows a "scholarly version of assassination," in very academic terms: something brief and cruel, like "oddly overestimated"; "*discutable*" (debatable; the French); "*ganz abwegig*" (totally misguided; the Germans).

In the *Discourse on Method* not a single author is quoted, even though Descartes considered himself part of a critical community and expected its members to express their opinion of his work. He maintained an active philosophical correspondence (six of the eleven volumes of his works, in Adam and Tannery's edition). He was possibly the first author in history to give an interview in order to answer a list of questions (April 16, 1648: *Entretien avec Burman*). All of which makes it even more remarkable that he never quotes anyone. It's a critique of the academic world. His position is Socratic: Don't come to me with quotes from Aristotle, without thinking for yourself, observing, conducting experiments, weighing merits. Don't read me without criticizing me, either. "I request all those who may have any objections to make to my doctrine to take the trouble of forwarding these to my publisher."

The citation as scientific proof (even when accompanied by irreverent commentary) has a nobility (the critical tradition, culture as conversation) that's lacking in the citation as a formality observed to comply with admission requirements. There's something valid and educational in making sure that each discipline's bibliographic sources are handled capably by all participants. But citations as credentials are no longer citations as proof or illustration of assertions.

From the misuse of citations pressed into service as credentials one arrives at a greater offense: false credentials. "People often pretend to have read things they haven't. There are thirty-year-olds who quote more books in their works than could be read in several centuries" (Nicolas de Malebranche, *De la recherche de la verité,* 1674; cited by Antoine Compagnon, *La seconde main ou le travail de la citation*).

The final (or most recent) abuse is the postmodern superseding of all of these concerns: There's no point in discussing misuse, plagiarism, or rehashed work, because all authors are second-degree authors, all text is intertextual. Nothing is original: everything published is a fabric of quotations, allusions, interventions, parodies, homages, with no origin or center. The death of the Creator ultimately implies the death of the creator. Which doesn't prevent Michel Foucault and Jacques Derrida from claiming authorship of their books, defending their author's rights, collecting royalties, and developing a reputation among their followers as brilliant original thinkers. In practice, the doctrine is advantageously reversed: if there is no creator, everything is permitted. The second author is as much an author as the first, as original as the first, with all the same rights.

The forgiving nod of postmodernism has served to legitimize many pedestrian or injurious transformations that pass for creation today. Borges presciently mocked what was to come when he invented a character (Pierre Menard) who becomes the author of *Don Quixote* simply by transcribing it.

But there are artists who take this seriously and present a tampered-with work by someone else as their own.

Similarly, the publication of semiological studies describing how texts refer to one another and mutually modify one another has given rise to a whole academic industry, documented by Udo J. Hebel in *Intertextuality, Allusion, and Quotation: An International Bibliography of Critical Studies,* which I haven't read and don't need to read in order to cite in postmodern fashion.

CHAPTER 5
Accumulable Quotations

TO QUOTE IS TO CONVERSE, adopt a tradition, acknowledge previous works. "We're like dwarfs on the shoulders of giants," said Bernard of Chartres; "and so able to see more." And yet there are ways of climbing that help us look better, not see better. The universities (which grew out of the cathedrals' scholastic centers, like the school at Chartres, which Bernard headed) transformed knowledge into credentials which became indispensable for advancement. Quotations became points to be accumulated for the benefit of the quoter and the person quoted.

Unlike the desire for fame, which is age-old, the desire to be quoted seems to be a modern phenomenon. Evidence abounds beginning in the eighteenth century. Gulliver talks about a professor who "made me great acknowledgments for communicating these observations, and promised to make honorable mention of me in his treatise" (Swift, *Gulliver's Travels*, part III, chap. 6). In 1757, a celebratory prologue by Richard Saunders (Benjamin Franklin's pen name) appears in *Poor Richard's Almanack* (upon the 25th anniversary of its hugely successful publication), complaining that the author isn't quoted. "Courteous reader, I have heard that nothing gives an author so great pleasure, as to find his works respectfully quoted by other learned authors. This pleasure I have seldom enjoyed; for though I have been, if I may say it without vanity, an eminent author [...] no other author has taken the least notice of me, so that did not my writings produce me some solid pudding, the great deficiency of praise would have quite discouraged me" (*Writings*).

Franklin might have been satisfied when some of the maxims he wrote for his lucrative almanac (like "Time is money") became popular sayings. But he yearned for the applause of his colleagues, as authors often do, even when they're successful. In 1977, after Romain Gary had been successful for many years, he complained bitterly to Bernard-Henri Lévy that no one ever quoted him: They read me, they admire me, they steal my discoveries, but they don't quote me; and "all that matters is whether you're quoted or not" (*Les aventures de la liberté*). This bitterness can give way to cynicism, as in two regrettable episodes recorded in the diary of Adolfo Bioy Casares (*Descanso de caminantes*). Letter from a well-known writer

(p. 79): "Oscar tells me there'll be an article of yours in *Claudia*. I'll be looking out for it to see how you repay the flattering references to you in mine." A sad sketch of a writer who has just died (p. 466): "Funny, sweet. She said that if I wrote a review of one of her novels, she would sleep with me. I wrote it and we slept together, making a joke of it." With melancholy irony, Don Marquis mocks his own desire: "Writing a book of poetry is like dropping a rose petal down the Grand Canyon and waiting for the echo" (Tony Augarde, *The Oxford Dictionary of Modern Quotations*).

The ontological urge to be quoted in order to achieve reality arose earlier than economic imperatives, and runs deeper. But it ultimately became part of the quest for income, when the résumé market, which sprang up in the twentieth century, established a criterion that didn't exist in Franklin's times: "Credentials are money." In the Middle Ages, scholars calculated acts of merit on indulgence days; in the twentieth century they set up precise systems for the measurement of résumé qualifications. These calculations are as unreal as religious reckonings, but just as the market for indulgences produced perfectly real benefits, the résumé market now offers tangible rewards.

In 1955, Eugene Garfield proposed the creation of a Science Citation Index, as a heuristic resource that would avoid the complications of subject indexes. Instead of classifying and grouping scientific articles by subject (which is difficult), each article would be indexed according to the articles cited by the author (easy). The clusters of references would provide the practical equivalent of a subject index. This approach (explained by the subtitle: "Citation Indexes for Science: A New Dimension in Documentation through Association of Ideas," *Science*, July 15, 1955) had further applications. It would be possible to see the reaction to each article—an important feature when it came to qualifying or discrediting its arguments. Meanwhile, it would serve as an individual clipping service for authors, who "like to see how their works are received." Also, the impact of an article, author, journal, or institution could be measured by the number of times it was cited.

This final innovation caused a revolution. The subtle methodology of baseball statistics, which permits the quantification and comparison of sports feats, was applied to science. The Institute for Scientific Information (www.isinet.com), created by Garfield in 1964, sells this information and has had an influence similar to that of the organizing committee of the Olympic Games. It's a world nexus of referencing and accounting that changes the nature of the competition by merely existing. Today, miraculous advances and mediocre rehashings alike are measured by what they have in com-

mon: the number of citations they generate —
which has sparked a multitude of tricks to inflate
the number, because the quantity of citations influ-
ences the income levels of people and institutions.

No Luther has emerged to rail against this new
market of indulgences (social critic Ivan Illich
comes closest), but there is much to criticize about
it. For example: Articles may credit twenty co-
authors, each of whom, naturally, adds the article
to his résumé, with the institutions benefiting as
well from an increase of their per capita output.
The significance of heading the list of contributors
is debated: Is it a concrete acknowledgment of
having made the main contribution to the work or
an institutional prerogative, like being department
head? Ugly stories circulate about those who buy
mentions by the lavish deployment of their social
and physical graces. Mechanical systems are
invented to filter out those who always appear as
co-authors, never as sole authors or at the head of
lists. There's talk about schemes of the "you quote
me, I'll quote you" variety, as well as about the
systematic exclusion of many journals, especially
those from underdeveloped countries. It's recognized that in the most thoroughly threshed fields
(where there are thousands of researchers, not
dozens), more researchers cite one another, to the
benefit of all involved. Studies are undertaken of
authors who raise their score by quoting them-

selves. According to Blaise Cronin (*The Citation Process: The Role and the Significance of Citations in Scientific Communication*), Jon Weiner wittily calculated Garfield's own self-citation rate (an extremely high 79%).

Soon the need arose for a Social Sciences Citation Index and an Arts and Humanities Citation Index. The three have created a "high culture" phenomenon equivalent to the concentration of bestsellers and the star system in film, television, and sports. They reflect and reinforce the problem of measuring quality in culture. Before there was a permanent competition based on numbers (because measurements didn't exist), comparisons between "advanced" and "backward" countries were based on qualitative assessments, which gave much more weight to the quality of daily life and the development of literature, the arts, and the sciences. Beginning in the middle of the twentieth century, GDP statistics, ratings, numbers of copies sold, and the Citation Index focused the attention on figures that had nothing to do with quality.

It goes without saying that measurements don't affect those who know how to read them without being distracted or letting themselves be fooled. If a reader finds a book on Amazon.com whose sales ranking is two million (meaning that two million other books have sold more copies), he won't sneer at it; he'll be grateful that a text so little in demand is available at all, when the business concentrates on the top sellers. Similarly, if he admires an obscure writer, he'll simply say so when he talks to other readers, when he writes (if he writes), and when he publishes (if he publishes). And yet, many people aren't independent thinkers, but let themselves be swayed by statistical judgments arrived at mechanically, by ignorant or biased consensus, the party line, the conventionalism of success. It's a reality that can't be ignored, because its effects are felt in the cultural world and it skews judgments about quality.

George Steiner has pointed out that great cultures can't exist without great teachers (*Lessons of the Masters*). But it's difficult to measure what the conversation of a great teacher produces. This leads to the devaluation of oral production and the elevation of written production, which seems more objective, but the problem persists. The calculation of how much has been written does nothing to distinguish mediocre production from miraculous production. It serves to enhance the seeming accomplishments of those who have nothing to say (orally or in writing) and who now, by publishing, seem very productive. When it becomes clear that written production is deceptive, another measure is added: production that gets cited, which is also deceptive, because there are all kinds of tricks for generating citations. Then computational filters are invented to filter self-citations or citations by colleagues from the same institution — which doesn't prevent new schemes from being devised, nor does it ultimately help us to hear those who have something to say.

In this cult of the résumé, the respect of others, bureaucratic ascent, income, and even self-confidence depend on favorable citations. Each act, person, and institution is rated. Living is a perpetual Final Judgment. Not being mentioned is worse than never having been born; it means suffering the excommunication that precedes eternal damnation. Many ridiculous mentions are made of those who devotedly swept the lab, typed the paper, helped with one thing or another, simply out of a desire to rescue them from limbo. And just as with films and their interminable lists of participants, a friendly or sympathetic mention can become something demanded, haggled over, traded. These fierce disputes over credit have something about them of the desperate struggle for existence, with those who receive mention surviving and everyone else disappearing.

Production has always been a miracle, as evidenced by the onlookers who surround the glassblower as the incandescent glass takes shape. This is a miracle that is prolonged in the use and contemplation of the craftsman's piece: "The pitcher of water or wine in the center of the table is a point of confluence, a little sun that unites the dinner guests" (Octavio Paz, *In Praise of Hands: Contemporary Crafts of the World*). These miracles of production and conviviality exist in their own world and are beyond compare. The revelation that produces a turn of phrase by simply setting two words together is in some way analogous to the miracle that produces a sudden and inspired turn of the craftsman's hand. But some analogies are dangerous. Metaphorical comparisons enrich the things being compared: the hand of the glass-blower also writes, the hand of the writer is also physically productive. And yet, numerical comparisons impoverish, reducing the two objects of comparison to an inferior third thing: the simple number of pieces produced. How can we reduce miracles to measurable, accumulable units?

Measuring is desirable in many circumstances, so long as the measurement doesn't interfere with the production of miraculous work, or worse, replace it. But measurements are fascinating in and of themselves. There's something magical about numbers, as the Pythagoreans knew. They are mysteriously perfect abstractions, exciting even when it's not clear what they represent. An infatuation with numbers can lead to the distortion of many realities, out of an eagerness to go further, to break all the records in an abstract world of comparisons.

There's something fascinating about the eagerness to accumulate (money, accomplishments, indulgences, fame, power, advancement, knowledge, recognition, or simply good deeds) that goes far beyond the sinister passions Marx attributed to capitalists, and Freud to the anal personality type. It's the same desire for the seemingly unattainable — salvation, ultimate fulfillment — seen in those who aspire to sainthood, beauty, and truth. The terrible austerity that Simone Weil imposed on herself, Samuel Beckett's literary radicalism, the tireless searching of Goethe's Faust, inspire more respect than other forms of dissatisfaction, but spring from the same root: the thirst for more.

To make a fair comparison of intellectual output, the common denominator should be the miracle. But how to compare one miracle to another? The revelations in Edward Hopper and Gunther Gerszo's paintings: are they comparable? What do they have in common that can be measured? Since this is a problem no one knows how to solve, miracles are measured in square feet, number of exhibitions, market value, medals, prizes, appointments, accumulated citations — just like in the Middle Ages, when acts of merit were accumulated (or indulgences bought) to get into heaven.

CHAPTER 6

At the Feet of the Footnotes*

HYPOTHETICAL STAGES in the rise of the footnote:

1. The first Christians enthrone the page. It's the codex—bound rectangular pages, like all books since then—that's best suited to liturgy, study, and meditation, not the scroll.[1] The first notes appear in the margins, simple abbreviations that indicate complementary passages: cross-references to aid the reader who pauses, compares, ponders.[2] We're in the monastic world of prayer

---

*Paper presented at the Third International Colloquium of the Asterisk, on "The Rise of the Footnote: Carnivalesque Inversion from Bottom to Top."

[1] Guglielmo Cavallo, "Between Volumen and Codex: Reading in the Roman World" in Guglielmo Cavallo and Roger Chartier, *History of Reading in the West,* University of Massachusetts Press, 1999.

[2] Richard H. Rouse, Mary A. Rouse, "Concordances et index," in Henri-Jean Martin, Jean Vezin, *Mise en page et mise en texte du livre manuscrit,* Éditions du Cercle de la Librairie-Promodis, 1990.

and slow, reflective reading in small doses. The note is marginal, anonymous. It isn't at the foot of the page, but it does kneel.

2. In the Middle Ages, the secondary apparatus of devotional reading paves the way for the academic industry.[3] Intervention is no longer anonymous and now aspires to be explication or commentary. In modern times, it becomes a separate voice that accompanies the text, and even interrupts it or judges it (from offstage, but in the role of reader's accomplice and interlocutor, in opposition to the voice of the text, which is reduced to background music as the notes are read). This requires more space than the narrow side-margins, especially where the annotated lines are close together. Widening the margins would waste paper. The solution is to break in with a symbol (no longer in the margin but invading the text) that directs the reader to a footnote, where the second author can expound at length at the first author's expense, even mocking him, but always in symbolic prostration at his feet.[4] The

[3] Ivan Illich, *In the Vineyard of the Text: A Commentary to Hugh's* Didascalicon, University of Chicago Press, 1993.

[4] Anthony Grafton, *The Footnote*: A Curious History,* Harvard University Press, 1997. Chuck Zerby, *The Devil's Details: A History of Footnotes*,* Invisible Cities Press, 2001.

academic deceitfulness of the *I* subordinate to the famous author is transferred to journalism: the interviewer who abases himself, feigning admiration, to better exhibit the interviewee.

3. The proliferation of symbols makes it necessary to number them, until the ballooning presence of the second author and his showy critical apparatus bury the first author. The apparatus no longer facilitates the reading of the first author; instead, the original text is reduced to a pretext: a kind of long, all-encompassing reference for the real text, which is the commentary. Once the first voice is silenced, the second sees itself as the Holy Spirit, dictating the Bible. It comes to feel worthy of footnotes of its own: self-references, derogatory commentary on others' commentary, narcissistic musings before meta-discursive mirrors (see my first version of this "Note," written seven years before Grafton published the first version of his book[5]).

---

[5] The first version of this "Note" ("Nota al pie de las notas al pie*") was published in *La Jornada Semanal*, V, 212, October 9, 1988, with the asterisk already in place. The title and asterisk of Grafton's book seem to be the work of the editor, because the copyright page announces a forthcoming French edition titled *Les origines tragiques de l'érudition: Une histoire de la note en bas de page,* and mentions a previous German edition with the title *Die tragischen Ursprünge der deutschen Fussnote,* 1995.

4. Of course the first author can play at the same game, without waiting for his commentators: he can step outside himself and write a metatext to his own text. But what's the advantage of interrupting the reader, inserting asterisks or numbers and diverting the flow of the narrative to scholarly notes that must be read separately? If the additions aren't commentary by someone else (or by the same author as someone else, twenty years later), notes to one's own text can serve to introduce a pause, a second voice, or a change of tone in the same voice. But most of the time, this is neither intended nor desirable; and if it is intended, it can be achieved without notes. Such is the function (incidentally) of meta-discursive sentences. Such is the function of prosodic and syntactic devices that allow one to switch rhythm or tone. Such is the function of punctuation (parentheses, not to mention the simple comma or new paragraph). Centuries before musical notation, punctuation (like typography later on) was used to convey meanings that in speech are distinguished by modulations in voice and gesture.[6]

Stepping outside oneself can be useful for the purposes of composing a text in two voices by the same author, voices that fit together and mutually

[6]Malcolm B. Parkes, *Pause and Effect: Punctuation in the West*, University of California Press, 1993.

enrich each other. It's also possible that a second author might achieve something similar, taking the second voice like a *basso continuo,* if he knows how to accompany. But usually the reader is in the uncomfortable situation of listening to two voices talking at the same time; the second interrupting the first, even when it doesn't have much to say. Noël Coward complained: "Having to read a footnote resembles having to go downstairs to answer the door while in the midst of making love."[7]

Practical aside: It's debated whether footnotes should go on the same page, at the end of the chapter, or at the end of the book. For the reader's sake, the author's notes would ideally be intercalated into the text, precisely where and when they need to be read (**if** they need to be read; many are superfluous). When the notes are by someone else, or when the author himself (for the reader's benefit) discovers that the text would be more readable and attractive in two voices, they should go at the foot of the same page. It's ridiculous to have to look for them, flipping back and forth and trying to make sense of the fact that there are twenty or thirty notes numbered "1.", instead of a single running count. To save themselves a few hours, authors and editors inconsiderately cause the general reader to waste one hundred times as long.

[7]Quoted by Grafton, p. 70.

(To calculate this, all one has to do is multiply, say, the ten seconds lost in finding each note by the number of notes by the number of readers, which equals hundreds of hours.) Reading pleasure shouldn't be sacrificed for editorial convenience.

5. And so we reach the loftiest heights: the asterisk in the title.

One would have to comb through the academic journals to discover who the first person was to come up with such a brilliantly kitschy idea: starting the notes before the text itself. The pedantry of footnotes goes to the author's head, makes him drunk on his own importance, and the title is crowned with an asterisk—like the Christmas star, which rises in the East bringing tidings of a birth worthy of universal attention.

This kind of preciousness has less to do with the reader's enjoyment than with the author's publicity interests. Once attention has been drawn to the honor of having been invited to read a paper at such and such congress, or to the imminent launch of a book, it's of secondary importance whether the piece is read.

CHAPTER 7
Quotable People

IT'S NATURAL FOR AUTHORS to quote other authors, because literary traditions are conversations.

It wasn't always so. In prehistoric works, mention is made of gods or characters who said one thing or another, but no authors are quoted. The creator of the text doesn't consider himself part of a conversation, even though he is. In contrast, Aristotle mentions or discusses some hundred authors, which is what happens when there's a proliferation of texts that are no longer sacred, texts that are bought and sold in the Athenian marketplace, and that readers discuss, praising or criticizing them.

To quote is to link conversations, to introduce two friends who might discover a common bond. An author who quotes another author recognizes a work worthy of consideration, not just in general, but specifically on the point under discussion. This recognition ranges from homage (or criticism) to the simple fairness of not ignoring a fellow author, let alone making surreptitious use of his work. A friendly regard for the reader is demonstrated by the passing on of useful information and the introduction of authors of interest.

But quoting (or not) can be less noble: a calculated act for the benefit of the writer, not the reader-friend or the author quoted. Manuals explaining how to use quotations, and conduct codes covering plagiarism, co-authorship, and slander, don't usually include a chapter of schemes for benefiting oneself at minimal cost. It might begin like this:

Before showing anyone what you intend to publish, make sure that you've obeyed the following rules:

1. *Don't* mention, much less favorably:
   (a) enemies or competitors of anyone who must give his approval in order for the text to be published (even if the omission is unforgivable in the context);
   (b) authors not recognized as specialists (even though you've made use of their ideas);
   (c) superseded specialists, who used to be fashionable but are no longer quoted by any respectable member of the guild;
   (d) authors who are too popular and are quoted by amateurs, not connoisseurs;

even more so if they write in second-rank
countries, let alone for newspapers;

(e) authors who are unpopular because of
their scandalous reputation, incorrect
ideas, or association with the worst kind of
groups.

If a mention is inevitable, clearly manifest your
opposition or elegant disdain. At the very least,
protect yourself with handy qualifications.

2. *Do* mention, and lavishly:
   (a) the reigning deities of the speciality, the
   institution, the country, the moment;
   (b) the magnanimous people or institutions
   who authorized or sponsored the publication (even though they may have hesi-
   tated, haggled, or imposed humiliating
   conditions);
   (c) the authors and texts that serve as pass-
   words to success, proving that you belong,
   that you're up-to-date and on the right side;
   (d) the critics and editors who will probably
   review or assign reviews of your book, not
   to mention those who might consider it for
   a prize, put it on reading lists, give you a
   scholarship, nominate you for grants, or
   give you a job;

(e) and, of course, your bosses, friends, teachers, and colleagues, especially those you're indebted to, according to the Golden Rule: If you quote me, I'll quote you.

These rules may not appear in any handbook, but writers do follow them. I once read a manuscript that was submitted to a magazine and rejected, as is so often the case with unsolicited pieces, even though the author made laudatory mention of several of the magazine's regular contributors. A while later the piece appeared in another magazine, and no mention was made in it of the contributors to the first magazine, which struck me as interesting. Had the rules changed? No. The references had changed. Conveniently rewritten in places, the article now made laudatory mention of the regular contributors to the other magazine.

Quotable names vary from one magazine to the next, one organization to the next, one country to the next. They vary over time, too. In later works (or in new editions of previous works), mentions, dedications, and co-authors appear and disappear depending on the circumstances:

↬ A is just beginning to publish, and quotes B, who is already well-respected in certain circles that matter to A. Time passes and B is eclipsed (A stops quoting him), or B becomes a celebrity (A boasts of being among the first to recognize his greatness). It may also happen that A becomes more famous than B and stops quoting him, either because he doesn't need him anymore or because he identifies so much with what he's learned from B that now it feels like his own, and he can't go on thanking B forever. Indexers can track these evolutions and observe, for example, that A's latest book, which is derived entirely from B's work, doesn't even mention him, although A quoted B profusely in his first books.

✌ M receives letters from N, so full of usable remarks that he uses them. But they can't be cited, because they're private, although naturally M cites many of N's published works. When N dies, the mentions decrease; and when N's complete works are being prepared and M is asked for copies of the letters, he says he doesn't have them. He lost them when he moved house.

✌ P has much in common with the famous Q, but not his talent. He runs the risk of being considered a kind of third-rate Q. To avoid this, he presents himself as the polar opposite of Q. If he pulls it off, he'll be quoted everywhere, because insecure people who want to avoid trouble or need to seem impartial will mention him when they quote Q, so that no one can say they're taking sides.

⁀ R makes many clever remarks in meetings
with his magazine colleagues and they use his
ideas without crediting him, because you can't cite
a conversation. They're all dead now and there's
no way to prove it, but it's easy to imagine S publishing an article using one of R's remarks, fully
conscious that he's borrowing from R. All of S's
colleagues realize it too, but since R doesn't complain, everyone assumes that he understands it as
an homage and a demonstration of his influence,
not as a theft. It's easy to imagine, too, that as time
goes by and others praise S for his clever idea, S
starts to think he came up with it himself; in any
case, it's too late for painful explanations. Finally
the day comes when R needs his old idea for a
piece and doesn't know what to do, since S has
already gotten so much attention for the same
idea. If he uses it now, everyone will think it's S's,
and it might seem like plagiarism. He chooses to
laugh it off with an elegant solution: quote the
impressive article by S, who doesn't even see the
irony, and thanks him for the mention!

⁀ In his first interview, the young poet says
he owes everything to the beloved bards of his
native land, to the excellent poet who is his mentor
and teacher, and to the great men of the capital.
Thirty years later, he explains his origins: Homer,
Virgil, and Dante.

At Paul Dry Books our aim is to publish lively books "to awaken, delight, & educate," and to spark conversation among friends. Our titles include works of fiction and nonfiction—biography, memoirs, history, and essays. We also publish the Nautilus Series for Young Adults, great writing for avid readers of all ages.

To receive our catalog, return this card or e-mail us at pdb@pauldrybooks.com. You can see excerpts, reviews, news about our authors, and articles about us and our books at www.pauldrybooks.com. If you like our books, tell your friends about them.

Name

Address

City, State, Zip Code

Email (the best way for us to communicate with each other)

Book title

BOOKS TO AWAKEN, DELIGHT, & EDUCATE

PAUL DRY BOOKS, INC.

1616 WALNUT STREET, SUITE 808

PHILADELPHIA, PA 19103

All the ignoble ways of mentioning (or not mentioning) someone are explained by a very simple calculation: the benefit to the mentioner (not the mentionee and not the reader) versus the cost of the mention (or failure to mention). For the purposes of this calculation, the benefit doesn't involve helping the reader or giving credit to the author who's being mentioned, but accrediting oneself by the mention. The cost is the risk of being discredited by crediting the author, or giving too much credit, or not enough, or none at all.

In general, the deck of mentions and omissions is shuffled conservatively. Cost considerations (the risks of quoting or not quoting) prevail over considerations of benefit (self-flattery, self-ingratiation, belonging). One can calculate how much each mention and each omission will cost, and how much it will produce. Some omissions are costly: they're to be avoided. Some mentions are flattering, or can be had for cheap, or pay off in other ways and aren't risky at all: they'll abound. Some mentions entail little gain and great risks: they'll never be made. Some omissions short-change reality, are of little service to the reader, and are unfair to those omitted, but cost nothing at all: they'll be perpetrated.

The cost/benefit analysis changes according to circumstances. Authors gradually become mentionable as they become safe bets, especially when their names acquire momentum by inertia: when many people begin to mention them because many others already have. Key to this inertia is the amplifying effect produced by journalists and cultural officials, whose many tasks give them no time to read, but who desperately need a list of safe bets in order to do their job.

Who are the top people in a certain field? Who should be interviewed, photographed, spotlighted, quoted, considered for such and such a prize, honor, or appointment, anthologized, nominated to a particular academy, sent to represent the country, included in dictionaries, mentioned in histories of the country, or at least in histories of the field? It's hard to know, without the ability to judge and the time required to undertake a general review. But the list is urgently needed, and it's drawn up (justly or unjustly) in the heat of the moment. Whether someone is included or excluded due to the ignorance of the compilers, friendship or enmity, prior commitment, whim, oversight, chance, or scheming, inertia makes it likely that proper choices and errors alike will be perpetuated. Thus the established names begin to be consolidated into a canon of safe bets.

And the canon has its effects. X? Who is he, if no one mentions him? Y? Maybe he's a mediocrity, as you say (I haven't read him, nor would I have the time to just now); but if he's mentioned frequently, if he won such-and-such a prize, if he belongs to such and such a group, appears on television and in the papers, is great friends with Z, and is a charming (or fearsome) person, he can't be ignored.

Who'll take the trouble to make his own list, after reading all the quotables and omissibles? Plenty of time, enthusiasm, courage, strong opinions, and a certain authority are needed to go against the flow, to eliminate or add names. And for what, in the end? To be left in the uncomfortable position of making those who didn't do the work—those who didn't have the time, the ability, or the desire to make trouble for themselves—uncomfortable. The generally accepted list represents not just truth, but peace: the agreed-upon truth that no one wants to reexamine after so many unpleasant episodes; the convenient truth, settled upon for the sake of expediency, stability, and smooth social interactions. One can't organize a work agenda, an election, a tribute, a dinner, with a perpetually shifting roster of who's in and who's out. They are who they are. If you want to be a bore and say that the Great X is only mediocre and Hayseed Y is the next Aristotle, go ahead. We'll all laugh at you.

Praise to those who do the work! To those who quote to give, not to receive. To those who enjoy the conversation and enrich it, introducing potential friends to one another.

CHAPTER 8
The Odds
Against Reading

READING, WHICH IS THE CENTER of literary life, is a mental and solitary activity, although it can be experienced as a dialogue, and even involve a certain physical liveliness. José Vasconcelos talked about books that we read standing up, that move us to act, take notes, consult a dictionary, see our surroundings with new eyes. To share that excitement, to talk about the experience of reading, about what a book says and how it says it, what you liked or what was disappointing, makes public and private life more intelligent.

But there are other expanses of the literary world, some so peripheral that reading becomes superfluous. Or so hectic that there's no time for reading. Paradoxically, the activities that dominate "literary life" are those that flourish without anyone needing to read at all.

1. Conducting a literary social life without reading, which entails:

⌁ Learning the names of authors and books from quick summaries that tell you what you need to know and what to think; from encyclopedia entries, book jackets, album covers, museum plaques, theater programs, advertisements, news, interviews, stray remarks, or overheard opinions. This is information you can use, information that will help you take part in the conversation, learn the territory, and make choices, because there isn't time to read everything. These briefings can function as a quick preview, which in many cases is all you need.

⌁ Getting an idea of a book (preferably in a nice edition) from its jacket, typography, and illustrations. Even better, having books around at home, to keep you company and to be shown off, along with photographs, signed editions, and mementos of well-known writers: decorative objects that lend cultural warmth (not just prestige), create atmosphere, and don't need to be read.

⌁ Getting to know authors by their social trappings. Being up to date on the gossip about their social lives, sex lives, and quarrels, the vicissitudes of fame, power, and fortune. Even better, addressing them by their first names at gatherings that could lead to long acquaintanceship, if not necessarily to the reading of their books.

There are always shy people who are embarrassed to attend a dinner in celebration of an author's latest book without having read the book. But more worldly people realize that the important thing is the toasting, the excitement, the sense of being part of a cultured circle, the witty remarks, the gossip: what the party says, not what the book says.

There are plenty of innocents, too, who make excuses for themselves by claiming that books are expensive and hard to find (they tried four bookstores!) and they don't have time to read. Never mind that the book would've cost less than the dinner, and that it would've been quicker to read it than to get together, celebrate, and go home.

In social life, all that matters is social life, not reading, even though there may be talk of books. When it comes to authors, the important thing is to get to know them, not read them: to rub shoulders with the Establishment; to let fall a seemingly inadvertent remark that occasions the startled response, "So you know him!"

Public events tend to be less entertaining than private dinners but more democratic: an opportunity for those who aren't invited to the dinners.

There's the author—you can see him, maybe even ask him questions, feel part of the literary life. Perhaps (although the likelihood is low) you might go so far as to buy one of his books, especially if he signs it, to display at home as a conversation piece. But if it were possible to know how many people read the book, before or after the event, and not just from among the public, but among the organizers and presenters, too, the real purpose of the event would become clear.

What matters when it comes to book parties is the party, not the book. What matters is the theatrical staging of a ceremony that serves to give the writer a social presence, with advertisements and notices in the newspapers, on the radio, and on television. Which in no way requires the participants to have read the book or to plan to read it. All that matters is spreading the news that the book exists, the author exists, the publishing house exists, the distinguished officiants of the ceremony and the institution where it's held exist, for the benefit of all concerned. The important thing is what the ceremony says, not what the book says.

2. Publishing news about authors, not reading them

In total, the newspapers in Mexico City publish more cultural pages than the New York City or

Paris papers. This is a relatively recent phenomenon. At first it seemed a step forward, and it is: for
everything designed to make reading unnecessary.
The cultural pages create buzz for authors, books,
and institutions; all that's needed to achieve this are
headlines and photographs, so that not only does
one not have to read the books, one doesn't have to
read the articles (which are usually uninteresting).
The important thing is the size of the headlines, the
amount of space allotted, the placement, the color:
essentially, the editor's decision to showcase a book
or to ignore it. The reviews themselves—many of
which are just summaries of advertisements, invitations, jacket copy, and publicity releases—are
irrelevant. Intelligent, well-written pieces by one
author who's read another, who knows what he's
talking about, and who expresses his honest opinion, are few and far between.

When there were fewer cultural sections, the
best writers wrote book reviews and the talented
young writers fought for the privilege of taking
turns with the established writers, writing pieces
that didn't pay much but did furnish them with
an abundant supply of books so they could read,
read, read. Unfortunately, the proliferation of cultural pages hasn't been accompanied by a proliferation of top-notch writers. To fill all those pages,
writers with media degrees have appeared, so
steeped in classes on film, television, radio, news-

papers, and magazines; so conscious of the new
media as an improvement on books ("a picture is
worth a thousand words"); so absorbed in the bus-
tle of daily life that they don't have time to read.

How can those who don't read rank literary
achievement? By assuming that true achievement
lies not in miraculous texts but in the social events
that celebrate them. By ranking these social events
in the same way that weddings, official ceremonies, and the commercial launches of new products
are ranked; not literarily, in the way outstanding
or disappointing works are ranked. If the outstanding work appears without creating a buzz, it
isn't news, although word travels among those
who do read. Conversely, a disappointing work,
written, published, and presented by prestigious
people and institutions, appears in the papers and
on television, even though disappointment travels
by word of mouth among those who do read.

Media buzz may — but doesn't necessarily —
reflect word of mouth. In the first place, buzz
tends to be positive. The cultural apparatus doesn't
raise a clamor to announce that it's made a mistake. But the main reason is that buzz doesn't require reading. It may be started in various ways
(by friends, by happenstance, through self-promotion) and thereafter bounce from one media source
to another. How do newspapers rank authors? By
the space that other papers allot them. By their

71

presence on the radio and on television. By their titles and ranks, especially in the cultural apparatus. By jacket copy and press releases. In good publicity heaven, whatsoever hath the most buzz, to it shall be given more buzz (noise is news: it generates additional noise), but whatsoever hath not, from it shall be taken away even that it hath (it seems to deserve it).

But where does literary life take place if not on the page? There's almost nothing about that in the cultural sections. It isn't news, it isn't gossip, it isn't a photographable image. Also, it takes time. It's faster to interview a writer than to read his books. Talking to him, taping him, photographing him, is more interesting than spending hours, days, and weeks reading him. Publishing an interview is like inviting the public to the private dinners of the Establishment—even more so if the interviewer manages to slink into private chambers, with the journalistic instincts of a Mata Hari, professing love for the interviewee until a comment is teased out that sinks him.

Cultural journalism has become an extension of entertainment reporting, and it's delivered in the same package: soft news. What matters are the headlines, the photographs, the interviews, and the star gossip, all of which keep us up-to-date and furnish us with cultural conversation while freeing us from the need to read.

3. Consecrating without reading

People with experience on committees know how easy it is to participate without having done the work; how naïve it is to assume that everyone has read or studied the documents required to vote and reach a decision. The same thing happens in sessions to choose new members of august academies, to award honors, distinctions, and prizes: all without reading.

To simplify, let's ignore the cases where too much rests on extraliterary matters, because then, by definition, it's unnecessary to read the work. The clear-cut cases, in which juries aren't subject to any kind of pressure but are saddled with inhuman responsibilities, are more indicative. If the candidate is a charming dinner companion, if he appears in the papers and on television, if he has an impressive résumé (that is, if other juries have already given him prizes, honors, and appointments), if I've been informed of his many merits, it's absurd that at this very inconvenient moment I should drop all of my work at hand to read his books, and all the books by all the other candidates! So the voting is based on hearsay, with the voters relying on the jury members who did the work. Of course, if no one did it, and the previous juries didn't either, the results can be embarrassing: Important works are ignored; mediocre novels are celebrated; more and more interests are created by buzz, rather than by reading.

The perfect mediocrity, persistent and likable, may make a career for himself like that described by Jules Renard (*Journal*). He is awarded his first prize because everyone says "Poor man, he's never won a thing!" He gets the second because he's just received the first. He gets the third because he already has two, and the fourth because he demands it. He gets the fifth because after so many prizes, not giving him this one would raise eyebrows (it might be thought that he was excluded for ideological reasons or out of prejudice against minorities). He gets the sixth because it's become a habit to give him prizes. The rest are an avalanche. Society, institutions, the State, reward themselves by elevating writers to the level of sacred monsters.

To correct the errors and omissions of the canon, intrepid, public-spirited readers with talent and amazing luck are needed, because once a mediocre work has been consecrated, once it's been given the stamp of approval by people and institutions of substance, it's hardly reasonable to expect they'll change their views. The reasonable thing is to assume that the naysayer is an eccentric with a twisted take on what he reads, that he's inept or motivated by undisclosable reasons.

In 1918, who would have dared to think, let alone say, that a young poet praised by José Vasconcelos and Carlos Pellicer, prologued by Rafael López and Antonio Castro Leal, reviewed in the *New York Times* and the *Saturday Evening Post,* wasn't important for what he had written, but for the attendant buzz? To win that absurd battle, one would have had to read him seriously, be prepared to challenge the positive consensus, make all the necessary efforts, and find support for one's opinions — a project as tiresome, unlikely, and dubious as finding a budget, assistants, laboratories, to refute the scientific experiments of a Nobel Prize winner. Today no one talks about Pedro Requena Legarreta (1893–1918). Nor does anyone read him. He went from being famous, without being read, to being dismissed, without being read.

Huberto Batis tells a depressing story. Teaching a class of literature students in their last year of college, a suspicion made him ask: How many of you have read Ramón López Velarde? General silence, and a single hand was raised, accompanied by a dispiriting explanation: family ties in the poet's homeland. In other disciplines and countries, similar stories are told. A notable one (because it reveals how bureaucratic the academic world has become, its members modeling themselves on corporate executives rather than readers) begins with a thesis advisor's surprise at some remark: How can you say that, when your bibliography includes such and such a book? Have you really read it? Brief executive response: Not personally.

Bad prose has become almost a requirement in the social sciences. Historians, sociologists, and psychologists who write too well are suspected of being superficial. But in literary studies it's a contradiction. Bad writing on belles lettres reveals scant understanding of the literary game, an inability to read one's own and others' texts. And yet, taste, cunning, the passion for reading (always praiseworthy) aren't needed in order to accumulate résumé capital in academia.

4. Publishing without reading

An excellent Dutch editor, Carlos Lohlé, told me about his rise from top executive of a European publishing house to small-time editor in Buenos Aires. The European house, a multinational corporation, got into trouble by publishing a book that was full of unforgivable nonsense. A thorough investigation was launched in every department, and it turned out that no one had read it.

"How can we publish books no one has read? Because we aren't oriented toward reading, but toward achieving goals of growth, production, sales, profitability. If I personally read all the books I published, how many could I publish? Extremely few, because in order to publish one I have to read ten; and if I don't have time to read more than two or three a week, I can't publish more than one a month."

Admirably, Lohlé accepted the facts and resigned in order to start a publishing house where he could personally vouch for each book as a reader rather than as an executive, who, when asked whether he's read a book, must confess: Not personally.

It goes without saying that his calculations apply to everyone in the book world: readers, booksellers, librarians, promoters, distributors, editors, journalists, critics, professors, researchers, authors. And that every aberration derives from the same crushing reality: no one can read enough. In order for the machine to keep running, it must be geared to the notion that reading is highly advisable, but not required.

To express a dinner-party opinion about recent literary, intellectual, or artistic developments when it's taken for granted that everyone's read everything, from the classics onward, one needs to have kept up with the news, not read books. Simply to read everything written by our acquaintances, we'd have to devote ourselves solely to that; or retreat from society, give up all friendships, and live in the desert; or not read, but mingle with writers and get to know their books by title, jacket copy, interviews, honors, and awards. The writers can hardly be offended, because they do the same thing themselves. In the mutual exchange of books, the important thing is the formal gesture: what the act of remembering a friend or acquaintance says, not what the book itself says.

The extreme case is when authors haven't read what they publish. This is true of some very busy individuals who are nevertheless eager to see their names on books. It is true of collections of academic papers that even the other paper-givers didn't listen to and that no one will read, because they're printed to boost the credentials of the participants and institutions involved. It is true across the wide world of the non-book, in which volumes are designed and produced by someone directing the work of assistants, rather than written. It is true of some prolific writers who write without stopping or reading, not even to correct their mistakes.

When Brezhnev was head of the Supreme Soviet, a book appeared under his name that was translated into dozens of languages, presented at countless roundtables, and glowingly reviewed all over the planet, although it's possible that no one read it: not the "author," or his editors, presenters, or commentators. Many of the extremely expensive books published by large institutions and businesses to celebrate themselves, or as Christmas presents, share the same fate: they're cellulose transformed into printed paper, soon to become cellulose again. But it doesn't matter. Inside the echo chamber, the true purpose of this cellulose, recycled over and over again, is to generate echoes, not reading.

Some monks believe that prayer sustains the world: that at any given moment there's always at least one pious soul praying from the depths of his heart, and that's why the world doesn't dissolve into nothingness. We believe, innocently, that if the world of books isn't reduced to the circulation of cellulose, it's because there's always some real reader out there.

CHAPTER 9

Three Concepts
of Complete Works

IN APRIL 1846, at the age of twenty-four, Gustave
Flaubert wrote to his friend Maxime du Camp:
"Wouldn't it be an excellent idea for some brave
soul to publish nothing until he was fifty, and then
to suddenly present his complete works one fine
day and add nothing else." "An artist who was
truly an artist and only for his own sake." No
worries about building a career, or paying court
in order to be accepted; no disputes with editors,
or nods to critics, or bribes to purchase fame.

The project is so striking (the true artist sets
out to create a work, not a career) that it over-
shadows an even greater imperative: the building
of a complete works. To publish anything before
it's completed is like publishing half a story, and to
add anything is like prolonging a story that's
already finished.

Flaubert's bold proposal was inspired by Balzac,
who dreamed of a world of interconnected novels,

with characters appearing in supporting roles in some novels and as protagonists in others, the same situations reemerging from new perspectives. He spoke about this idea in 1834, gave it form in a collection of 17 volumes published between 1842 and 1848 (under the general title *The Human Comedy*) and announced its expansion to 137 novels, of which he ultimately wrote 85.

What paved the way for Balzac and Flaubert's grandiose conception of a complete works? It's hard to say. To explore the matter, one must begin by recognizing it, acknowledging its importance, placing it center stage. Who created the first complete works? Was it a project of the author or the editor? Is it a genre, a philological effort, a line of products in the book business? The question changes as it evolves within the framework of a broader story: that of the text and the author. The earlier stages can only be recognized retrospectively and by forcing the matter. Can one speak of the complete works of Moses or Homer?

The great anonymous texts immortalize the legendary figures whose deeds they record (*Gilgamesh*, XVIII cent. B.C.). Next the figure of the author is immortalized, endowed with legendary attributes (Moses, Homer). The texts themselves come to be seen as incredible deeds of literary genius, to be carefully preserved, collected, and reproduced after the author's death

(Plato's posthumous custodianship of the work of Antimachus, IV cent. B.C.). Finally, with the rise of the printing press, authors consecrated in their own lifetimes see the publication of their collected works (Congreve, XVIII cent.) if the publisher finds enough readers willing to subscribe and pledge to purchase a copy. Complete works are a tribute to society and a luxury item, even when no one reads them.

Society feels exalted by its exalted authors. Authors who are legendary for their work end up attracting attention in and of themselves, at the expense of the public's interest in actually reading what they've written. Interest comes to depend less on the texts and more on the fact that they're by someone famous. (A mediocre text or a great painting rises or falls in esteem when it's discovered that it's by someone else, not the person originally believed to be its creator.) Consecration leads authors to see themselves from the perspective of fame, of posterity, to let themselves be carried away by the idea of themselves as figures of legend, resisting it (when the role isn't to their liking) or appropriating it as something of their own creation. The image that the public has of an author (or that the author himself would like to foster) may shape the development of his work and even his life. Byron, for example, adopted his legendary romantic persona not only in poems but in his private life, playing the role of hero and reaping the consequences in the public arena (scandal, the armed struggle against Turkish imperialism), in the marketplace (bestsellerdom), and in his personal finances (Robert Escarpit, *De quoi vivait Byron?*). Upon the arrival of the press and television, this role-playing feeds into great projects of self-creation, with the author marketing himself like a famous brand.

At the same time, more ambitious projects arise: the artistic positioning of an author's complete works as a single work, the whole greater than its parts (Balzac, XIX cent.). This is very different (and, in the case of Flaubert, clearly opposed) to the notion of the artist as persona, his true work his public career.

1. Complete works as posthumous concern

Unlike in contemporary literature (which is dominated by the presence of the author to the point that it becomes, in large part, a literature of the *I*), in oral literature and in the early days of written literature, the text was dominant, the author "absent," anonymous, or at a mythical remove. The preservation of the integrity of the text, its reproduction from memory, its transcription by scribes, the process of obtaining, collecting, conserving, classifying, and consulting it in the form of scrolls and codices, the textual criticism, the study, the preparation of critical editions: it's all a posthumous project, not part of the author's creative initiative. It's the words of the tribe preserved in memory. It's the collection of scrolls kept in a library. It's the transcription, criticism, and scholarly publication of the texts of the sacred, legendary, anonymous author. It's the posthumous homage to the works of an admired author.

An important example of the evolution of the editorial process occurs in Antimachus, in whom three different moments coincide: oral reproduction, written circulation, and the posthumous custodianship of the work of a respected author. First, Antimachus was the disciple of a Homeric rhapsode (reciter); then Homer's editor (scribe); and finally an admired poet whose poems (lost today) were in turn compiled by Heraclides Ponticus at the urging of Plato. In other words, Antimachus participates in the oral preservation of the "complete works" of Homer; he participates in the transcribed publication of those same works, ordered by Peisistratus; and, as author in his own right, he's one of the first to have his reputation cemented by a posthumous collected works. Heraclides made a special trip to Knossos to seek out Antimachus's writings, copy them, compile them, and bring them back to the Academy library. This was a veneration that had begun in life, as Alfonso

Reyes writes, based on Cicero's account: "When Antimachus read his poem [the epic *Thebais*] in public, all those present disappeared one by one until only Plato was left. 'It doesn't matter!' said the poet. 'I value Plato's opinion over that of a thousand others!' And he continued his recitation" (*La crítica en la edad ateniense*).

Barring the discovery of some prior example, the complete works of Antimachus (IV cent. B.C.) are the first to be attributed to a known author, and they were compiled after his death, as an editorial project. The initiative (similar to Plato's own "edition" of the "complete works" of Socrates, with written dialogues recreating the subject's oral arguments and public persona) seems to have no antecedents. It's a stretch to see a parallel in the transcription, editing, and study of the Pentateuch in the tenth century B.C. (if the Pentateuch is considered to be the complete works of Moses); or in the curatorial and editorial works attributed to Confucius (551–479 B.C.), which came much later and weren't the complete works of an author but miscellaneous compilations (documentary, ritual, chronological, anthological); or in the transcription of the different oral versions of the *Iliad* and the *Odyssey* (if they are considered to be the complete works of Homer).

The editorial efforts of Plato's Academy were expanded at the Lyceum of Aristotle and perfected at the Library in Alexandria, where Aristarchus completed the first critical edition of a text: He gathered the existing transcriptions of the *Iliad* and the *Odyssey*, matched them verse by verse, compared the variants, and chose for each line the hexameter that seemed most convincing (II cent. B.C.).

2. Complete works as publishing strategy

The second conception of a complete works arises as the commercial project of a publisher who's a contemporary of the author.

The appearance of the printing press (XV cent.) reduced the cost of books that had previously been copied by hand (the Bible, missals, breviaries, Biblical commentaries, theological treatises, Greek and Latin classics) and created the possibility of reaching a larger public. This possibility — afforded by new technologies and the prosperity of a growing middle class — was manifested in a few bestsellers, beginning with the Bible; but was limited (in terms of the number of copies sold) for the simple reason that publishers were printing the same books that had been copied in the Middle Ages, or new books that the humanists had begun to produce — translations of classics, collections of aphorisms, dictionaries, philosophical dialogues, marvelous satires like Erasmus's bestseller

In Praise of Folly. The prospect of reaching wider markets encouraged the creation of less specialized content for a larger potential audience: books of popular science, encyclopedias, manuals, comedies, novels, pamphlets, satirical and libertine texts, literary almanacs. It also provided the necessary conditions for the emergence of writers articulating the new bourgeois consciousness.

It was this new conversation, in addition to technology and prosperity, that brought the publishing business to a notable peak in the eighteenth century, and led to the early canonization of authors like William Congreve (1670–1729), creator of the comedy of manners, who at the age of forty published his complete works as the finishing touch to a dramatic career that had ceased to interest him. A publisher had issued a pirated single-volume collection of five of Congreve's pieces, and that spurred a legitimate publisher to convince the author to collect all of his work, which Congreve carefully revised for the reading public. It sold well (Julie Stone Peters, *Congreve, the Drama, and the Printed Word*).

Voltaire was less fortunate. A publisher convinced the author to put together a complete works, but once the publisher received the package, he resold it instead of publishing it. Fortunately, the buyer was Beaumarchais, who issued a nice posthumous edition (Robert Darnton, *The*

Business of Enlightenment: A Publishing History of the Encyclopédie, *1775–1800*).

In contrast, Goethe, celebrated at twenty-five as the author of a bestseller, *The Sorrows of Young Werther* (1774), with which many young readers identified to the point of suicide, could be crowned at fifty-eight as a living legend upon the publication of his complete works, which he personally oversaw. Also, as letters and contracts show, both Goethe and his publisher kept close track of the enterprise, which proceeded through three further editions (one of them pirated) in the author's lifetime (Siegfried Unseld, *Goethe and His Publishers*).

3. Complete works as creative ambition

Balzac had a similar business experience with his publishers, but he was inspired to give it a creative twist, formulating a third conception of complete works: the artistic project of an author who integrates the whole of what he's written with what he plans to write. The idea had been formulated before, in a note by Jean Paul Richter (unpublished until the twentieth century): "I'd like to make one big novel out of all my novels" (*Ideen-Gewimmel*, a selection of notes translated as *Être là dans l'existence* by Pierre Deshusses). In Spanish, there was the case of Valle-Inclán (1866–1936). Rafael Dieste, who as a young man attended literary gatherings presided over by Valle-Inclán, described to me the great importance Valle-Inclán assigned to the structure of each book and the whole of his work. Dieste also described the problems Valle-Inclán faced upon writing a new text, when it became evident that he should tinker with some book that had already been published, even if he had to readjust the whole of his work; his refusal to listen to criticism from friends and editors on this point; and finally, his choice to publish his complete works himself, at his own expense, in order to shape his artistic vision with no hindrances.

For legal and cataloging purposes, an author's complete works are like one more work, although obviously none of the twenty-six volumes that make up Reyes's oeuvre could possibly contain his Complete Works (a Russellian paradox, jokingly resolved by Augusto Monterroso with the publication of his *Complete Works ... and Other Stories*). Nevertheless, it's clear (as in Russell) that artistically there is no paradox: complete works exist as a whole on a different level, their wholeness unlike that of the individual works which constitute them. Just as a memorable sentence can be a work in and of itself and exist independently of the poem, story, or essay of which it forms part—which, in its turn, can (and should) be a work in its own right, separate from the book that contains it and which, in *its* turn, can (or should) be a polished whole, not just a jumble of poems, stories, essays —so too the entirety of an author's books can (should?) be a work in its own right.

It's clear that a story is a work with its own scope and sharply defined boundaries, and it's clear that stories have been assembled haphazardly into collections since antiquity. And yet the idea of a story collection that isn't a simple assemblage but rather an independent work is a recent creative project in literary history, possibly devised by Balzac in 1830, when he collected six long stories or short novels under the general title *Scenes from Private Life*. Thus was born his great plan to publish 137 novels as a single work.

For the ambitious young Flaubert, complete works were the culmination that brought creative order (and, in the process, the fullest significance) to the chapters, paragraphs, sentences, and words of which his books were composed. Projects of this nature are, of course, impossible, not only because they're too ambitious, but also because there's something somnambulant about the creative evolution of a work. The author (like every conscious self) is born halfway there, en route, and his awakening is always relative. Lucidity is never absolute, let alone prior to the fact and part of the creative process. Lucidity is made in the making. The author arises from the work. Those who know exactly what they want have yet to awaken.

Flaubert's challenge is valuable for reasons that have nothing to do with preconceived plans to be followed. When he presumes that publication should be postponed until the author is in possession of his complete works, his lack of moderation is practical, because the changing of a single comma here triggers a new change there; the effects of modifying a paragraph in one book are felt in another; each new text composed makes it necessary to recalibrate the whole. To conceive of the complete works as a constellation of interactive parts is to pursue a heuristic ideal of search by trial and error, to let oneself be carried away by the creative impulse but to continuously submit the results to critical appraisal; to try to understand what was written, to eliminate or correct what makes no sense, and to be guided by the requirements of the existing material toward a happy encounter (unexpected and yet expected), toward the revelation of something new and habitable that makes everything harmonious, up to the last irreplaceable word, syllable, comma.

Naturally, this happy harmony is easier to achieve in a poem or a perfect page, like so many by Reyes, than over the whole of the thirteen or fourteen thousand pages that make up his oeuvre.

Complete works as a literary genre (the perfect constellation) are an impossible goal. But the rigorous ideal of a body of work fully governed by the pleasure of reading is one that may be shared equally by the creator in the process of discovery (as he strives to understand what he's brought to life, and what still demands to be brought to life), the posthumous editor (as he works to assemble what's been scattered), and the critical reader (as he attempts to appreciate the whole).

CHAPTER 10

Foolishly Complete Works

WHAT TO INCLUDE in a complete works? In what order? Raw or cooked (and if cooked, how)? To what extent should the editor intervene? What is the author's work and what isn't?

Negligence (the authors', their families', posterity's), fires, wars, sackings, dust, damp, and bugs have destroyed works that we don't even know existed. What wouldn't we give today for any scrap of the ancients that might be recovered: texts, fragments, manuscripts, documents, statements, portraits, belongings?

The new form of negligence is to preserve everything. Monumental works are published that aren't meant to be read, or even consulted. They're pharaohs' tombs, a grand landmark for tourists, but little else. They block access to their treasures and lay a curse on the bold reader who profanes their content. Unfortunately, it's the number of volumes and expensive binding that impress most, not the ease of reading. No critical judgment is needed to pile up everything vaguely related to the author until his work is buried in a crushing mass.

Accumulation may be inoffensive when it comes to the ancients, because few authors require more than one thousand pages, all told. But today there are authors under forty who've already written more than Plato, Cervantes, or Shakespeare and who file everything, so that even their laundry lists are available for publication. The exhaustive has become unmanageable.

In the first place, this is because readers' admiration has been contaminated by the worship of movie stars, pop stars, sports stars, political stars, and other performers, with all the attendant fetishes: the pen with which a bill was signed, the ball from a memorable game, the dress worn in such and such a film, autographs. The result is that many meaningless things are invested with meaning. Plato surely knew what Socrates ate for breakfast, but didn't consider it worth mentioning when weighed against his teachings. John didn't bother to record the words that Jesus wrote on the ground, words that caused the accusers of the adulterous woman to walk away instead of stoning her. In contrast, Boswell published fifteen hundred pages of anecdotes, letters, documents, and minutiae from Johnson's life, including everything he himself heard and observed, all the letters and documents he received from Johnson or others, and everything he was told. The cult of personality he established anticipated a common phenomenon today: readers who are more interested in gossip about writers than in reading them.

In the second place, authors themselves, since the eighteenth century (Rousseau, Johnson, Goethe), have encouraged the chronicling of their lives and the preservation of portraits, objects, documents. Some have even produced "original manuscripts" of published texts, to give as gifts or to sell. Bernard Shaw was so conscious of the value of his autograph that he tried not to write checks for small quantities, because they were never cashed (Maurice Colbourne, *The Real Bernard Shaw*). And today it's common for a celebrity's employees to sign contracts that prohibit them from exploiting their access in order to collect objects, take notes or pictures, make recordings, give interviews, or write memoirs about their experiences. Image control is now the same as control of a registered trademark: the celebrity's image is his own creation, property, and product, belonging only to him, not to any assistant. At the same time, tabloid journalism, the paparazzi, and all the vampires who feed off other people's lives try to besmirch the established image, pulling off a parasitic coup that generates its own celebrity and profits. An even more repugnant variation: the celebrity who shares the profits, entering into an agreement with the vampire to fake an accident or moment of distraction that yields scandalous photographs.

Third, relativism makes everything equal (or in other words, meaningless). When Plato doesn't report what Socrates had for breakfast, that's elitism. Even worse: rather than being considered impartial, he's accused of sacrificing Socratic reality to Platonic ideals. What right does he have to mention some things and omit others? Everything must be included, without value judgments. When Socrates (*Meno*), in full-on maieutic exchange, enters into a dialogue with a slave to help him unearth what he knows about geometry (without the benefit of an education), what he's doing is no more important than ordering breakfast from him.

Fourth, simple accumulation looks good. Whatever is "most complete" seems better. Quantity impresses, and anyone can appreciate it at first sight. Quality isn't as obvious, or as easy to appreciate. As if that weren't enough, quantity is easier to produce, less labor-intensive, cheaper, less risky than saying: Not this.

Fifth, technology offers more and more means of preservation and reproduction. Though it may be true that some new developments are counterproductive (acid paper: less durable than papyrus;

optical and magnetic recordings: less legible than a Sumerian tablet after twenty years), there's no doubt that our archiving potential has been greatly expanded thanks to the printing press, photography, audio recording, film, and the digital recording of texts, images, and sound. Techniques for the physical and chemical preservation of many materials have also been developed.

It would be a wonderful feat if today's technology had preserved every cultural achievement dating back to prehistoric times. In the complete works of humankind, none of the marvels now lost would be missing. But the most wonderful feat of all would be the ability to locate those marvels amid millions of tons of garbage. There are no machines capable of appreciating, distinguishing, or highlighting what's important, as the reporter who tapes a long interview realizes when he has to spend at least as many hours listening to it all again and selecting what's worthwhile. In the archives of Babel, all valuable works would be preserved, but they'd be as lost as if they didn't exist. An eternity would be needed to examine everything and discard, one by one, the infinite number of works that merit the eternal rest of perpetual obscurity.

Preserving everything is a form of negligence that causes a new kind of damage: the loss of what matters in a glut of the insignificant. To preserve everything is to lose everything. A misfiled document in a small archive can be recovered; but once it's been misplaced among millions of files, with no clue to its whereabouts, it's just like a document destroyed in a fire. For all intents and purposes, it doesn't exist anymore, although it may still be there physically.

Today there are thousands of closed-circuit cameras that constantly record what happens in banks, jewelry stores, jails. But what's recorded is so boring that the security guards get distracted. And once all those infinite recordings are filed, they hardly gain in interest. If there's no hint that somewhere, at some point, something important is going to happen (or has already happened), it's very difficult to notice it against a backdrop of insignificant detail.

The unbridled production and preservation of works, files, objects, and recordings demand a cultural Malthusianism. The desire to keep Mallarmé's letters, and even the envelopes on which he scrawled impromptu poems (easier to imitate than to translate) is understandable:

> Va-t'en, messager, il n'importe
> Par le tram, le coche ou le bac
> Rue, et 2, Gounod à la porte
> De notre Georges Rodenbach
>
> [Get out, dear courier, I implore
> you. Rollerskate and parachute fast track

to 2 Gounod Street, the door
of our George Rodenbach]*

But do these flashes of humor and creativity jus-
tify, as a general rule, the publication of every
envelope, every letter, by every poet? And why
stop at scrawlings on envelopes? All of daily life
can be creative. If Mallarmé were alive, wouldn't
it be best if reporters followed him constantly,
wherever he went, with tape recorders and cameras to film and document everything he did?

This relativism rejects involvement, masquer-
ading as respect, impartiality, asepsis. Yet it is,
in fact, a radical intervention, a dismissal of the
author and his work. If every word Mallarmé ever
wrote, anywhere and for whatever reason, must
be considered part of his work—as well as every
draft, unfinished text, rejected version, suppressed
paragraph, chapter, or book; every word that ever
came out of his mouth or passed through his mind;
every movement, gesture, and direct or indirect
expression of any sort; every portrait, filming, or
taping; every statement, review, or poem about
him—then the compiler's judgment overrides the
poet's judgment and destroys his work.

In the hands of the creator, the oeuvre emerges
as something significant from among a multitude

*Author's own imitation. TRANS.

of possibilities, words, elements, projects, materials, circumstances. It detaches itself from whatever it isn't. Michelangelo said, wisely, that every sculpture was contained within a marble block and his work was to carve away the excess. But the exhaustive compiler comes and gathers all the scraps from the workshop, rummaging even in the trash, and restores each chip to its place (after painstaking labors of verification), reconstructing the original blocks and obliterating the work, burying it in the insignificance of its origins.

It's like reducing *Autre éventail* (the poem by Mallarmé inspired by the poet's daughter fanning herself) to its biographical circumstances or to a list of words—like returning a word to the dictionary. What did Mallarmé do, after all? He selected 116 words from the repertoire of the French language, setting them in a particular order and eliminating all the rest. It may rightly be said that stray words don't have the same significance as those chosen and ordered in a masterful sequence. But therein lies the question. What is a work, and who may claim authorship of it?

Respect for a work demands that it be protected from secondary materials. Ideally, of course, the author himself would exclude what shouldn't be published. This is made simpler when he completes, corrects, and personally sees to the editing of his complete works, once he decides not to write more, like Congreve. But complications arise when his works aren't yet complete and he needs his files and drafts, the unpublished or published work that he plans to revise. If only someone would invent a computer connected to the brain that, at the moment of death, would destroy all the materials the author considered unworthy of publication but kept in order to revise. Meanwhile, it's naive to leave the task to posterity, because it's more than likely that no one will undertake it. Or that someone will undertake it reverently and clumsily. Or with an eye to their own interests, base or lofty. Or that they'll do a wonderful job, as has also happened.

Naturally, the author himself can do a bad job. It's been revealed that many admirable books were less than admirable before a great editor stepped in. In fact, brilliant editors like Ezra Pound or Maxwell Perkins have been the anonymous co-authors of great writers. But intervention accepted by the author isn't the same as posthumous intervention. The posthumous editor must place the author's creative wishes and the reader's interests over his own impulses as co-author. He can intervene (clearly indicating it when he does so) in the gray area between author and editor: fixing spelling (unless the author has expressed a clear preference, like Juan Ramón Jiménez, who

whimsically chose to replace all soft *g*s with *j*s);
correcting obvious slips; choosing titles and subti-
tles (for poems written in a period when the poet
wasn't titling his work, if tradition hasn't already
established titles for them, for example); settling
the order of pieces, the placement of notes, the
bibliography and the formatting of citations, the
indexes (if the author hasn't clearly specified
what he wants). When it comes to books of
poems, stories, essays, or fragments, one must
respect the order the author chose in the last version he assembled himself, even if his inclusions,
exclusions, or shufflings were mistakes. If the
editor has a deep familiarity with the work, if he
knew the author and understood what the author
wanted and didn't want, he can intervene more
boldly (if necessary, and indicating where he's
done so, of course): retouching, simplifying, or
rearranging so as to better express what the
author (not the editor) meant to express.

Interests should be ranked in order of prece-
dence when assembling an edition of a work. The
reader's interests come first. Then the author's.
Then those of the researcher, who needs to look
things up. Last should come those of the heirs,
publishers, patrons. The various interests may be
compatible, and ideally they should be, so that the
act of reading (the enactment of the work's true

glory) is facilitated; so that the publisher and editor shine professionally and win prestige and money; so that the researcher has a useful edition at his disposal; so that heirs, disciples, fellow countrymen, institutions, and the state all honor the work and life of the author, and thereby honor and benefit themselves as well. But where there's a conflict, the reader's interests should prevail.

Ideally, a single, multipurpose edition should be good enough for every type of reading. A discreet critical apparatus may suffice for the researcher, without hampering the common reader. But when that isn't possible, there should be different editions, each with a clearly defined purpose. A delightful reading experience, initial or repeated, makes its own design and production demands. The quick search for something read previously or required for research purposes—in the text or the critical apparatus—occasions other demands, compatible or not with the aforementioned.

Archival material must be separated from the works themselves. To give the two equal treatment is to diminish the work, to reduce it to the level of a document. Texts like the speeches or private poems of a politician, interesting only by virtue of their authorship (or their purported authorship), can be published as documents; the works of a real writer cannot. At the other extreme are the letters of Petrarch, collected, revised, and published by Petrarch himself. These aren't documentary texts, but rather a part of the oeuvre.

The rules should vary depending on the quantity of material. It's one thing to assemble a five-hundred page volume, and something entirely different to assemble fifty volumes of a thousand pages each. When everything fits into one volume and there are few supplementary documents, appending these doesn't skew the presentation of the work or get in the reader's way. When correspondence, papers, and documentation take up one hundred times as much space as the work itself, the work must be published separately, for the reader's sake. The remaining material (as well as the work itself) can be made available in an electronic edition, with the proper search tools for researchers' use. Without these tools and the corresponding indexes, the whole body of work becomes essentially inaccessible, like so many archives (personal or printed) that are no better than sealed boxes. The title on the spine and cover of each volume should make the contents plain and orient the reader. For the same reason, multi-volume complete works should have a general index of names, in addition to separate indexes for each volume. It's extremely irritating to search for the same thing in twenty indexes, volume by volume.

The ideal, of course, is for authors themselves to destroy a good part of their work and papers. Very few have anything important to add after their best thousand pages. None have anything to add after their best ten thousand. Few great poets write more than a hundred memorable poems. To bury a memorable text in a set of foolishly complete works is to destroy it. The reasonable thing is to destroy everything else.

CHAPTER 11

Classics and Bestsellers

LIVELY CONVERSATIONS can be struck up between strangers of very different backgrounds and cultures, with the most diverse interests. And yet a lively exchange is most easily sparked when people have some differences but also something in common: they've read the same book, listened to the same music, visited the same place, or seen the same film—though their perspectives are shaped by their divergent experiences, tastes, and opinions. Paradoxically, that's why modern abundance can impoverish the conversation. The explosion in the number of books and records available, the places we're able to visit, and the people we can get to know all make it harder to find common ground. On a long international flight, two readers seated next to each other may each have read hundreds of books without having read anything the other has.

When production was artisanal and there was little long-distance trade, local life was the norm, in communities where everyone knew everyone else and options were limited. Yet this situation, which lasted thousands of years, produced astonishing human achievement. People as emphatically free and creative as Socrates, Saint Paul, Leonardo, Shakespeare, Descartes, Bach, lived in conditions that seem backward today. Bach didn't have many economic options. Nor did he have many competitors. When musicians began to travel, record, be heard in the big cities, or on radio all over, the world was enriched by unlimited opportunities. From another point of view, though, it was also impoverished.

The shared experience of music (in the local choir, at evening gatherings of friends) involved musicians who were neighbors and who played for an audience made up largely of listeners who knew one another, many of whom sang, read music, played an instrument, or even composed. With the appearance of concert halls, tours, international fame, recordings, and broadcasts, the typical experience has become that of an anonymous, passive, not so knowledgeable audience watching a distant, specialized star, who is only passing through, and who must compete with many others, from all over the world and even from the past. Local audiences and celebrities disappear. Fame no longer springs from the epiphanies of shared music, but from international prizes, television appearances, box office sales.

The market broke the autarkies of local music. For musicians, it created unprecedented opportunities: mass audiences and international fame. Opportunities for all, in theory, although the drive for sales excludes most, leaving the also-rans in limbo, out of the major leagues and outside the realm of shared music. For the listener, now a consumer of global products and services, the options have expanded unimaginably—although his free time, attention span, and memory have not.

Today, the discography infinitely surpasses the options available a few centuries ago. But who can listen to so much music? The Library of Congress has millions of scores and recordings. It would take a fulltime listener centuries to listen even once to everything that exists now, and then all of eternity to listen to all the music constantly arriving, because more is composed and recorded each day than can be listened to in a day. And listening to something just once isn't listening.

Musicians complain that the larger public only listens to the same old things over and over again. It's an unreasonable complaint. No one listens to the same thing the second time, or even the hundredth time. It's even possible to judge the value of a work by the number of times it can profitably be listened to, looked at, reread. Today almost no one rereads, and worse, hardly anything is worth rereading. If only the larger public spent its time rereading the classics, even if just a small minority read contemporary authors. What's the advantage of consuming insignificant novelties over returning to the same old thing with new eyes? Paradoxically, the limited can be more enriching than the unlimited. Returning over and over again to the same thing (which isn't the same) is a surprising experience when it involves works that resist repetition, that have something to say the second time around, and the hundredth.

Classics book clubs, like those promoted by the Great Books Foundation (the brainchild of Mortimer Adler), transform the reader. Years after receiving a doctorate (under the direction of a Nobel Prize winner), a member of one of these clubs said that he owed more to the club than he owed to the doctorate. Constellations of great works and conversation with good readers help us to develop our imagination, intelligence, and sensibility; to ground ourselves and find our way; to be happy and to be *more*.

Conversation inspired by great works was essential for millennia, not just for personal development, but as a part of the creative tradition. Great creativity is born from critical rereading, and classics — books worthy of being reread, books that raise the level of consciousness and dreams —

spring from other classics. Creations that were pleasing and lingered in memory, creations worthy of being repeated, heard, read, seen, or refuted, gradually began to make up the traditional canon, as something alive, shared, renewable, growing. Then came authorities, orthodoxies, and politics, and an official canon was imposed. Then came the market.

Lists of classics, textbooks, and bestsellers reduce the infinite to a set of options within everyone's reach, facilitate conversation about shared experiences. They're something like the standardized system of weights and measures: they create commonality, references for understanding one another. But there's more than one way to set standards. Great works are fixed in the memory through many shared experiences, which shape the list of classics over years, centuries, and millennia. The canon, always open to debate, is established by readers who are respected by other readers. In contrast, required texts are imposed on us by authorities, and bestsellers are defined by last week's sales.

There are inevitable tensions between these forms of selection, because their criteria and results are different. All three are subject to criticism. None is infallible. It would be ideal if they coincided: if the classics were also bestsellers and required texts. It happens occasionally. The *Iliad* and the *Odyssey* were popular before Peisistratus made them school texts, and they ultimately became Western classics. *Don Quixote* was a bestseller before it became a classic. In practice, even the worst required texts and the worst bestsellers at least allow us to talk about the same things. But the classics are unrivaled in their importance. They've elevated the human species, sparking a conversation that grows richer over the course of centuries, in the most diverse surroundings. They're cultural genes, the unchanging source of many different varieties of personal, social, and historical fulfillment.

CHAPTER 12
Shelf Theory

IN THE OLD DAYS, shirts were handmade, and their reputation rested on the skill of the tailor and the caliber of his clients. Now shirts aren't even made by the stores that sell them. They're offered as part of a general selection of ready-made clothing, whose (impersonal) reputation derives from the brand and the name of the chain store that carries them.

How many brands of shirts can a store keep on its shelves? Very few. Taking into account that each supplier offers various models in various styles and colors and a full range of sizes, no store can carry dozens of brands. The chain makes a selection, which gives the selected ones an advantage: they're within sight and within reach. Anything not there might as well not exist. The customer's choice is restricted by the choice the store has already made.

How does the chain decide which brands will be given this advantage? By comparing their profitability per square foot. Since investment and costs are more or less proportional to the display space, the store analyzes sales and profits per square foot for each store, department, and product. Based on this data, it eliminates any products with poor yields, and evaluates suppliers who want in. The supplier has to prove that his merchandise will do good business for the store; he must also invest in publicity and finance the inventory, if not pay a monthly fee for shelf space. But how much does it cost to advertise in every city where the chain operates? Millions. Supposing that the advertising budget is five percent of sales, a million spent on publicity must be justified by twenty million in sales. If one then adds the investment necessary to finance inventory for hundreds of stores (which, in fact, treat the goods as if they're on consignment), the sums involved are prohibitive for almost any shirt maker.

And that's the point. Market oligopolies are organized to prevent just anyone from getting in. Imagine a country where there are thousands of shirt makers. Hundreds produce brands of their own, but almost all are unknown. They can't invest in becoming established names across the entire country, never mind the world. The leap to the major leagues isn't a question of quality, because quality can be achieved on a small scale. An unknown brand, even a shop that makes handmade shirts, may be superior in design, fabric, cut, service. The leap is a question of branding. Quality is necessary, but publicity and a presence on the shelf in top stores are most important. Few can make the jump with such formidable obstacles in the way.

Shelf space is selective for another, equally important, reason: the limitations of the consumer's decision-making ability. The abundance of possibility means a wealth of opportunity. One could even say that wealth is precisely that: unlimited possibility. But who can manage the unlimited? The possible excites us, dazzles us, makes us dizzy. In theory, our choices can be analyzed like any set of options. But it isn't easy to rank everything in order, not even coolly and unemotionally. And it's all the more difficult when one is touched by the promise of happiness, temptation, risk, madness.

The conventional wisdom of shopkeepers is to avoid overwhelming the customer with too many choices, because choosing is complicated and agonizing. Not even the most cool-headed purchaser (of whom there are few) always has the necessary information at hand to create a spreadsheet and make a calculated choice. Also, considering the information that must be obtained, the trouble taken, and the time and even stress of comparing and deciding, it's easier to choose among two or three options than among twenty or thirty.

This conventional wisdom was confirmed in experiments conducted by Sheena S. Iyengar and Mark R. Lepper ("When Choice Is Demotivating," *Journal of Personality and Social Psychology*, 2000, 995–1006). In the first, a sampling booth of jams was set up in a store, alternately offering six flavors or twenty-four. The results: the offer of twenty-four attracted more customers (145 vs. 104), but there wasn't much difference in the number of flavors tasted by each customer (1.5 vs. 1.4), although there was a significant difference in the number of purchases made. Those who tasted one or two flavors out of six made a purchase eight times as often as those who tasted one or two flavors out of twenty-four (31 vs. 4). On the basis of similar experiments, Iyengar and Lepper concluded that, when faced with *no choice, limited choice,* or *extended choice,* people buy more in the intermediate case. They are attracted by the greater number of options, but discouraged by the problem of choosing when there are too many options (*choice overload*). These conclusions refer, of course, to choices made without previous expression of preference. When the customer already knows what he wants, and won't make a purchase unless he finds it, the larger selection sells more (although not necessarily more per square foot), because it increases the likelihood that the person who comes looking for something specific will find what he wants.

Herbert A. Simon came to a similar conclusion about calculated choice in the work for which he received the Nobel Prize in economics. The models that serve to quantify rational selection are limited by the difficulties of analyzing reality (*bounded rationality*). Mathematically, it's easy to maximize a single variable, if reality lends itself to such a simple model. But with a model that takes into account simultaneous and conflicting criteria (three, for example: profits, prestige, and market penetration), the respective maximums for each don't coincide. One must seek an optimal point that reconciles the different demands. The problem is that the size and complexity of the necessary equations, the quantity of information required, and the methods, time, and costs of calculation can be disproportionate. One has to simplify and resign oneself to acceptable solutions (*satisficing*), even if they aren't perfect. This has long been understood in the wisdom of the saying: Better is the enemy of good.

The possible liberates and oppresses at the same time. In practice, the greatest freedom is not endless possibility. And this isn't only because of the excessive cost of making calculated choices in every case or the emotional confusion of not knowing how to choose, but because our experience of possibility changes. It stops being concrete (immersion in one experience or another, with all the practical consequences and resulting responsibilities) and becomes abstract: the distant contemplation of an infinite series. Endless possibility produces an illusory sense of freedom. Concrete freedom arises from the concrete experience of concrete possibilities, and since each possibility requires time and dedication, there must only be a few.

A talented, wealthy young man free to choose any profession might end up in mediocrity, not only because he's bewildered by the array of options, but because his experience of the possible doesn't materialize into commitments that require him to resolve concrete difficulties. Pure possibility isn't freedom yet. If he chooses to become an organist, many years of daily dealings with real keyboards, real interpretations, real composition exercises are required to achieve the freedom that comes with work: a concrete freedom in specific realms, not in everything. By the same token, although he is forced to subsist on poorly paid commissions and he dreams of unattainable freedom, if he immerses himself in real musical problems and passionately seeks creative solutions for them, he might become Bach in the end. He can turn his constraints into freedom.

There's yet another way of looking at limited capacity. Our attention span and memory are finite.

How many things can we watch or listen to at the same time? How many authors (cities, theories, sports, tools) can we know in depth? How many names (paintings, songs, faces, circumstances) can we remember? There are politicians who have an astounding capacity to instantly recognize hundreds of people, and even associate them with some detail about which they can make conversation. But in reality, they neither know these people nor are interested in them. They file them like cards in a Rolodex, and today they can shuffle them in databases so that, at the right dates, the computer sends out warm birthday wishes. To have dealings with thousands of people (as respectful and well-intentioned as the personal contact might be) is to treat them like abstractions. It's like seeing twenty cities in twenty days, or traveling around the world in a balloon: a bird's eye view. To see an infinite set of things, one has to see it from a distance, as an abstraction, like the camera shot that swoops up from a street in New York to a panoramic view of Manhattan, and then a distant view of the planet. The concrete disappears.

The shelf (the limited space we have available for concrete options) is a basic function of human life (commercial, psychological, administrative, vocational, artistic, social, romantic, cognitive); but its implications are different depending on the scale of operations. Our attention span, our memory, our capacity for analysis, learning, and creation don't grow when the scale of operations is large. Our options increase, which can be enriching. But our dealings with people and things change, which tends to be impoverishing. The concrete becomes mere possibility; the nearby becomes distant; the personal becomes impersonal. Names become abstract notions of anonymity or celebrity; shared existence becomes public relations.

Our limited capacity for contemplating multiple options isn't transformed when operations are on a large scale; it's exploited to the benefit of oligopolies and their products. When the thousands of local markets remain independent, there's a local supply of limited options, different in each place. When those markets join the global market, the infinite richness of world diversity becomes theoretically possible, but unmanageable in practical terms. Variety has exotic appeal, and sufficient demand where there are large concentrations of wealthy population. Beyond that, the oligopolies will take charge of cutting it down to what sells most per square foot. That's why small local markets still offer only a few choices, except that now they're the same choices everywhere.

CHAPTER 13

The Economics
of the Limelight

WE'RE ALL ACTORS AND SPECTATORS in daily life.
Roles vary depending on the social situation of
each participant and his personal character, but
also according to the number of participants.

At a table of two people, there's a single conversation. At a big table there are more conversations,
never mind at a cocktail party. But for one hundred people to take part in the same conversation,
silence must be requested, small conversations
suspended, and everyone must take turns speaking. And so the need emerges for a system of
microphone control. Even if this is managed with
parliamentary fairness (so that everyone is able to
talk, listen, and respond within time limits), the
average interaction becomes very passive. When
two people are in conversation, each one talks for
perhaps half the time. When there are a hundred,
in order to speak for one minute you have to listen
for ninety-nine. The larger the scale, the more the

situation deteriorates. Raising the number of participants increases passivity, turning actors into spectators even in symmetrical conditions. But it also destroys symmetry, for another reason.

In a small, stable community, everybody knows everybody else. Each participant knows the others' names, faces, voices, distinguishing traits, and circumstances by heart. But you can't know a million people. In order for so many to participate in a conversation, it wouldn't be enough simply to take turns talking for a millionth of the available time; the participants would have to be acquainted with one another, which is beyond their capacity.

The memory can retain dozens or hundreds of people, maybe even thousands, but no more. For this reason, the organizers of shows or political events (constrained, also, by the duration of the act) have to focus the spotlight on just a few people whom everyone knows. Mass communication imposes asymmetrical conditions: mired in anonymity, a million strangers listen to a few familiar protagonists.

Asymmetry is power, and power easily becomes a business. A familiar face can draw a crowd, as protagonists, organizers, advertisers, sponsors, and all those who aspire to influence well know. Charisma is a revelation for those who share the experience: an immediate culmination that's an end in itself and asks nothing more than to be

121

allowed to persist. But it's also tradable currency for the protagonists, their public ("I was there"), those interested in buying or selling influence, and the owners of the microphone. It's a power that's imposed by silencing small conversations, whether naturally (admiration causing us to stop talking to listen) or with attention-grabbing tricks, in authoritarian fashion or not.

There are natural leaders in small circles, and there are many ways for them to become known in broader circles: by chance (a good singer happens to be heard by someone in a position to advance his career), lucky timing (having something that appeals to a particular audience at a particular moment), unexpected opportunity (filling in for a star who gets sick), the creativity of organizers (who cast fresh lineups), vested interests (of those who hope to exert a specific influence), self-promotion (of those who want to make it to the top, even if they don't know what for, and even if it ends up being counterproductive). But each way involves different power equations.

In non-commercial spheres (political, academic, religious), there is an endless battle for the microphone, and the ownership situation is complex: Who has the right to the word in the name of the people, the truth, God? To seize the microphone is to seize power. That's why political, academic, and religious organizations are full of gossip about mafias—unofficial power structures with hidden interests that control the microphone and impose their will by underhanded means. The same tensions exist in commercial spheres, but aren't as strong, because profit making is an official aim for the formal power structures. Control of the microphone is in the hands of companies whose business consists of gathering large numbers of people to sell to advertisers. This means an attempt to balance the interests of the company, producers, stars, and sponsors. It's an oligopolistic process, because there aren't—nor can there be—too many protagonists known to the larger public. Nor are there many television networks or mass venues or organizers of huge events like entertainment companies, political parties, universities, and churches; nor is there all the time in the world to attract the spectator's attention.

There are many angles to the game, and the same person can shift from one role to another. The advertiser can act as producer, rent the microphone, recruit stars, and stage his own events. The star can rent the microphone himself, finance his own production, and sell sponsorship to advertisers. The media company can obtain political or economic favors, since it controls the microphone. Politicians, academics, and clergymen can come up with schemes to make the news and attract the cameras, or make money by renting out the microphone, or offer blessings—the people's, God's, or scientific truth's—in exchange for attention. Actors, singers, or commentators can become politicians or businessmen; businessmen can launch themselves as politicians, singers, or society figures who get their names in the paper. Asymmetry is a more or less transferable source of power, one that can be transported from one position to another. It capitalizes on the basic reality that only a few people are recognizable by the masses.

This also explains a genre that might seem like an exception to the rule: reality shows. Using strangers in attention-getting situations can be a great deal, because they're in an extremely weak bargaining position. They know that if they don't get exposure, they'll continue to languish in anonymity (which some of them will later remember longingly). They don't have audiences of their own. They're turned into stars (fleeting as their fame may be) by the sensational situations in which they're exhibited. The deals they negotiate aren't the same as the deals brokered by people who already have their own audiences, audiences that will be multiplied by the mass media. Those who are already stars in smaller venues bring their own capital (established name, legitimacy, acknowledged talent) for broader exploitation. This is an advantage for the organizer, but it costs money. Minor stars have something to gain (if in fact there is anything to gain) from exposure to a larger public, but they feel they deserve it, and bargain from that position.

Naturally, the unknowns who become knowns once they've gotten some exposure also come to feel as if they're worth something themselves, and therefore have a right to the microphone. But that doesn't happen overnight, and in the meantime they pay for their apprenticeship. Once they have power of their own, they join the oligopolistic bargaining, wielding whatever clout they've acquired.

In practice, in the short term (and even in the extremely short term, if they threaten not to sing just before the curtain goes up), stars may come out on top. In the medium term, it's the organizers who have the upper hand. They can impose conditions on the advertisers, especially in prime time. But in the end, the advertisers win out. They may even be able to veto one star or demand another. This situation creates the illusion that power or money can arbitrarily create stars, but that's an exaggeration. The public can be manipulated, but it ultimately retains the final power: to grant its attention or not.

Putting a group of unknowns on public display, preferably in scandalous and attention-grabbing circumstances, can be a good deal for the producers, because there are plenty of unknowns willing to exhibit themselves at low cost, and no lack of advertisers to pay for the audience thus assembled. It's also a good deal for those who exhibit themselves: they gain a sense of importance, cultivate a reputation, and improve their bargaining position. What's hardest to accept about this collective degradation is the role of the viewing public, who make the deal possible in the first place.

CHAPTER 14

The Rise of the Image

ADVERTISING INTENDED TO SELL a company's image, rather than cars or clearance sales or circus performances, emerged during the Second World War. The Pentagon was absorbing much of civil production, and many items were scarce or rationed: they sold themselves. Advertising agencies and media, seeing their income fall, convinced companies that they should at least trumpet their participation in the victory effort, projecting a loyal and patriotic image.

Advertising a company to win social goodwill rather than to sell a product gradually established itself as a specialty: public relations. It goes without saying that great leaders (military, political, religious) have always worked with symbols. Companies began to do the same in television commercials. It was such a novelty that their methods transformed the ancient management of symbols into political, religious, and institutional marketing.

It became fashionable to talk about "image." The concept wasn't unknown. According to the *Oxford English Dictionary*, "this sense developed from advertising parlance in the late 1950s"; but the *OED* also cites a previous usage by Chesterton in *All Things Considered*, 1908: "When courtiers sang the praises of a King they attributed to him things that were entirely improbable...Between the King and his public image there was really no relation." After that, it leaps ahead half a century to Galbraith, *The Affluent Society*, 1958: "The first task of the public relations man, on taking over a business client, is to 're-engineer' his image to include something besides the production of goods."

At the same time (also in the mid-twentieth century), television appeared, reinforcing this new image management with the rise of the visual. The importance of the visual in public space had been established in antiquity, with architecture and the torching of cities and buildings as expressions of power. But it reached its zenith in the twentieth century, with illustrated newspapers, film and newsreels, and finally television. The visual media transformed our sense of reality, and, ultimately, reality itself. Products that didn't lend themselves to mass sales or couldn't be conveyed in images over the course of a twenty-second commercial became relatively unimportant. The same fate befell institutions and people who couldn't be summed up in a phrase, or who didn't have anything to say to the general public, or who photographed badly. It happened with events. Whatever lacked mass interest, couldn't be simplified, or didn't generate striking images was lost from sight.

The media is oligopolic and oligopolizing. A few events, people, and products are spotlighted. Everything else remains in shadows. Once, when the head of the local bureau of the *New York Times* was asked why there were so few positive news stories about Mexico, he answered simply: "Because there's no market for them." But neither the *Times* nor the television gives the appearance of excluding anything, let alone bowing to the demands of the market. On the contrary, they seem to be mirrors of the world: complete panoramas. (The *Times* slogan is "All the news that's fit to print.") If something isn't there, it didn't happen, doesn't exist, or isn't important. That's why some people feel that if they don't appear in the media, they don't exist. A deep need to *be* makes them fight for attention. They need to appear on the screen to be real, to fully exist, to find fulfillment. But how can reality fit into twenty seconds?

The screen is a kind of Borgesian Aleph, where everything fits into a dot; an illusory vision of the fullness of life that transforms life. It spurs the fabrication of events, personalities, institutions, and products designed to generate powerfully symbolic, visual, simplified images of interest to a mass audience. Thus was born the business of staging and producing "events" engineered to be news, of "beauties" designed to be photogenic, of "personalities" molded to be mediagenic, of books written to be bestsellers.

The historian Daniel J. Boorstin (*The Image*, 1962) talks about these fabrications: the interview purposely sought to generate front-page quotes on a slow news day; the meeting organized not in order to conduct business but so that the press may have a photo opportunity; and even the article commissioned by *Reader's Digest* to be planted in another magazine, and then selected and summarized by the *Digest*. Once set in motion, artificial reality feeds on itself. A front page quote becomes news by virtue of being on the front page. A bestseller sells a lot more copies because it's already sold a lot. A celebrity is known for his most notable achievement: being very well known ("known for his well-knownness," as Boorstin says). Quote, book, or person: it isn't notable, it's simply in the spotlight. Boorstin begins with an eloquent anecdote about reality taking second place to the image. "Admiring friend: My, that's a beautiful baby you have there! Mother: Oh, that's nothing—you should see his photograph!"

According to Pliny (*Natural History*, book XXXV, paragraphs 86–87), Alexander so loved his concubine Pancaste and admired her beauty that he wanted to possess a nude portrait of her. But his friend Apelles, upon seeing her and painting her, couldn't help falling in love with her. When Alexander discovered this, he contained his rage and, in a magnanimous gesture, gave her to Apelles. Pliny emphasizes Alexander's command of himself and the greatness of his friendship. A modern reading would emphasize the ambiguous relationship between the two friends, the exchange of objects—the model in payment for the painting—and the preference for the image. ("You should see the painting!")

The age-old distrust of the power of images is a recognition of danger: the loss of a sense of reality, the preference for unreality. Names, mirrors, shadows, portraits, echoes, symbols: all these replicas of reality have inspired fascination and fear, if not outright prohibition. Karl Popper (*Knowledge and the Body-Mind Problem*) situates the appearance of these abstractions (which he calls World 3, as opposed to the subjective World 2 and the physical World 1) in the evolution of the species and presents the three worlds as interrelated but autonomous. Images enter the physical world and society's shared system of signs through the works of the creative imagination. But once created, these works alter their creators, society, and the physical world. Words, numbers, knowledge, ideas, myths, metaphors, scenes, paintings, devices, and tools change human life and the face of the earth. So it happens that unreality comes to have power over reality.

Reflections of life are disconcerting. The split is both real and unreal. It's a miraculous leap outside of life's immediate reality, permitting the creation of a new reality zone. It's the source of consciousness and culture: life seeing itself in the mirror and improving itself, making the world habitable on a higher level. But it distances us from immediate reality, which can be confusing. It promotes objectivity, critical thinking, freedom, but it can lead to fetishism, escapism, alienation.

This ambivalence is present in the Bible. The Bible says that man is made in the image and likeness of God (Genesis 1:26), which not only glorifies man, but also glorifies the concept of the image. And yet, the Bible forbids the making of images of God (Exodus 20:4), which represents not only a condemnation of idolatry, but also of the glorification of images. Judaism and Islam still obey this prohibition. Christianity obeyed it in the beginning, but worship later began of relics, images, and symbols, which brought about great tension and scandals. The iconoclasts managed to get the Byzantine emperor to prohibit images in the year 730, and set out to destroy those that already existed. But they were condemned by the Second Council of Nicaea (787), in the name of tradition and the distinction drawn by St. Basil in the fourth century: worship is not of the images here on earth, but of the original in heaven.

Although the glorification of the image has become universal, it's a historic fact that photography, illustrated papers, film, television, and online images spread from the Western world (not the Islamist or Buddhist worlds), which may be a function of the Greek and Christian attitude toward the image, an attitude that favored the development of a split life.

According to Jacques Le Goff (*Le Dieu du Moyen Age*), Christianity differs from the other monotheisms in its worship of a man who manifests the fullness of humanity in the image of God, because he is, in fact, God. This is also the root of the controversies about his duality. Radical monotheism (Judaism, Islam) can't accept the splitting of God, let alone his division into three entities (Father, Son, Holy Spirit): it seems like polytheism. Even within Christianity, the Eastern branch refuses to accept the claim of the Western branch that the Holy Spirit proceeds from both the Father and the Son; and although they venerate icons, they don't take kindly to sculpted figures. Among Christians in the West, many Protestants see the Catholic cult of the Virgin, the saints, and relics as polytheism.

It's confusing that man is created in the likeness of God, that the Father is incarnated in the Son, and that one particular man is the Son, while still being the carpenter known to his customers and friends. It's confusing to suggest that humankind should take the carpenter as a model for its own fulfillment, that it should strive to imitate Christ. The normal confusion when one reality stands for another (gold for value, wolf for demon, drink for happiness) is increased when the reality of one person is made to stand for another. An actor is a specific person, but also the character he represents. And here the confusion is even greater if, instead of a mask (as in Greek or Japanese theater), the actor uses his own face as expressive object. This is especially true in a close-up or nude scene. Who is portrayed? The actor, the character? Does the actor's naked body stop being his body and become mask or costume? Is his own self disembodied?

It's also confusing when one person represents another, the former assuming the latter's social duties. Who is the subject of his objective acts? Whose interests is he promoting: his own or those he represents? This becomes especially complicated if the proxy acts in the name of a collective "person" (the nation, an institution), invested with its authority. A single physical body is the representation of two persons: real and symbolic. (Or the other way around, as Ernst H. Kantorowicz has it in *The King's Two Bodies*.) And this double personality is the source of confusion and missteps, of madness and corruption, which are the professional maladies of power.

In religion, theater, politics, and the courts, reality is enhanced when one person represents another, but there's a risk that our sense of reality will be lost. To play a role, to represent someone else, is to identify with a phantom object modeled on the actions of a real subject who is transformed into someone other than himself. This identification is active on the part of the actor, the proxy, or the person invested with authority, but no less important or ambiguous on the part of the spectator who identifies with the religious, political, legendary, fictional, or media protagonist.

In everyday life, we all see ourselves in the mirror of others, as actors and spectators. Spontaneous, unconscious mimicry as a reflection of others' behavior (even in forms as basic as assuming the same facial expression as one's interlocutor) is a natural mechanism. It facilitates coordinated activity (the flight of cranes in formation), childhood development (apprenticeship by imitation),

and cultural development (the spreading of innovation by imitation, observed even in chim-
panzees). In human life, this biological mimicry,
based in the so-called mirror neurons that make us
feel we are doing what we see others doing, is
enhanced by the use of mirrors, photographs,
recordings, and our growing stockpile of symbolic
creations. Mythology, the epic, the theater, history, the study of peoples and animals, philosophy,
biography, the novel, and film are interesting for
many reasons, but they've always been of mimetic
interest as well. They allow us to see ourselves in
the mirror of others, to better understand and
enrich our own lives. They're repertoires of behav-
iors, characters, situations, destinies, ideals, analysis, and examples. A kind of canon of the possible,
imaginable, desirable life.

There are many explanations for the expulsion
of poets in Plato's *Republic*. The one offered by
Eric A. Havelock (*Preface to Plato*) emphasizes the
influence of Homer's and Hesiod's great poems in
everyday life, as a kind of *paideia*. They were like
poetic encyclopedias of proper conduct, models
for living that everyone knew by heart. (Many
people today still base their conduct on some popular slogan, on scenes from movies or novels, or
on the behavior of celebrities.) But when Plato
creates a mirror for life in the intellectual prose of
debate, what use do we have anymore for popular

verse? To cast oneself in the mold of great characters is to live an unexamined life. When life manages to be self-conceptualizing and self-critical, it rises to its highest level. Imaginary life that exerts an unexamined influence over real life—with stereotypes, and, even worse, bad examples—is undesirable, like an insidious textbook. After Socrates, poets are superfluous.

But not everyone has the ability or inclination to engage in abstract analysis. Nor is it easy to understand life in general, or our own in particular, without observing other lives. Reading, going to the movies, watching television, observing other people, listening to gossip, dreaming, and fantasizing have a genuine effect on our private lives, projecting their reflection on us. The example of other lives shapes self-conception (I'm like this or I'm like that), autobiography (personal stories and myths), critical—or exculpatory—self-examination, and general thought (in the form of maxims). The gossipy drama of gods, demigods, and protagonists from the Homeric poems; the drama of actors who bring the classic tradition of gossip to the screen (and fascinate in turn as new gods, demigods, and protagonists); the gossip of neighbors, colleagues, and friends; all the drama of other lives is not only imitated but observed as a mirroring of our own lives, as an object of concrete reflection, as a primitive form of theorizing.

All theory, like art, is a product of the imagination, a hypothetical fiction, a model, an image, a metaphor: an unreality that helps us understand reality. Theory is creation, no less free or more rigorous than poetry. And yet theory can't replace literature as a model for living. None of the social sciences has produced, or will produce, better descriptions of personal or social life than the novel. Some (a few) realities are better modeled on abstract theories; others (many) are better modeled after literature. Not only that: the theoretical models (like the literary models) depend on language. Their respective treatments of reality are different, but each is based on speech. Even mathematical formulations on the page or the blackboard are constructed, presented, and explained in words.

Leaving aside the question of the worth of a particular poem or theory, the real argument against Homer, film, or television is the same one that's been made against philosophy, science, and intellectualism: they encourage a dangerous fascination with unreality that distracts us from reality. Images and models (of every sort), institutions and products (of every sort), can be the source of liberating revelations or suffocating dependence.

People who appear on television—even if only on a reality show—seem more interesting, important, good-looking, and intelligent, even to those who know them and never saw anything special about them before. More than one fan would be unable to recognize the actors he watches on screen if he met them working in an office, with no makeup or glamorous lighting. In everyday life, there are plenty of noteworthy people of admirable character, fascinating beauty, or superior intelligence who have reality on their side but not image, and thus they go unnoticed by fools who worship "success." The idolatry of images makes us blind to the miracles of reality.

CHAPTER 15

The Secret of Fame

GLORY SHINES UNBIDDEN, seizes our attention, speaks for itself. Fame follows on the heels of glory. It is simply talk, invocation of the miracle, even by those who never witnessed it.

Fame and *glory* are used as synonyms, but they aren't quite the same. The Indo-European root *bhâ* has two varieties of derivatives: those that refer to speaking (like *fame, ineffable*) and those that refer to shining (like *beacon, diaphanous*). According to Pierre Chantraine (*Dictionnaire étymologique de la langue grecque*), the two senses may have been confused from the beginning. Days are called diaphanous, but so is reasoning, as if the diaphanousness of day were a kind of eloquence and the clarity of reasoning a kind of transparency. As Tomás Segovia puts it in *Anagnórisis*:

> The day
> is so beautiful
> it can't lie

A day of spectacular diaphanous beauty is glorious, not famous, because its glory is immediate, ephemeral, inseparable from the display itself. Its beauty is not the fame of a place or name blindly repeated to refer to glories that are taken for granted but that are not visible before us. Present glory is a form of revelation, like beauty, truth, authenticity, heroism. It distracts, interrupts, suspends all action. It inspires contemplation. It speaks to us, leaves us mute, but also gives us something to talk about. It may occur in natural phenomena, personal acts, works of art, with the effect that we are shaken from the ordinary and reality appears to us as a revelation.

A great work of art disconnects us from immediate reality, and at the same time centers it and centers us. It lightens our load so we can return to reality feeling refreshed and freer, able to see our surroundings with new eyes. The great works of art are glorious, even though they're objects, because they have an innate shine. People, too, can radiate glory in some of their actions, private or public, like marvels of nature or great works of art. But better to put it the other way around: great works of art are analogous in some way to what's impressive about nature and people. They suffer when compared to living glory (natural or personal), which surpasses any work of art as an experience of reality. But they have the advantage

141

of crystallizing the miraculous, unlike days and people, which are easily blurred.

Trapping the miraculous in a poem, painting, or sonata, is a stroke of luck, greatly to be wished for. Out of words, pigments, or sounds, a zone of freedom is created, a wellspring of happiness for the creator who contemplates it for the first time, as well as for all those who happen by and are able to see the miracle. It's natural for this shared glory to become famous. Nevertheless, many join in the praise because of the reputation the object has acquired, not because they see the miracle. They have eyes and ears for what others are saying, not for the work itself. Even worse, the fame of the work is transferred onto its creator, as if he were the marvelous object, not his work—which is like negating the work that was the source of his fame and negating him as a person: he isn't an object, he's a subject. A glorious work (famous or not) is glorious in itself, as an embodiment of fulfillment, freedom, and joy. In contrast, for the artist to be trapped in the cage of fame as a (supposedly miraculous) object is an undesirable loss of freedom, a regrettable confusion.

Miracles in real life may be confused with their re-creation in art. Tales around the bonfire, dramas on stage, novels, and movies seem fascinating and real. Of course, a wonderful play is another kind of miracle, but not the original one. The actor in the play is not the real protagonist, but another person, a performer. But the confusion may be carried further. In their real lives, the author and the actors of a miracle on stage may deserve fame, but they are not the miracle. The original miracle, the re-created one, and the creator and performers of the re-creation are three different realities.

One may assume that tales of memorable deeds began to be told in ancient times, as family stories recounting what our grandparents did or said. These recollections became myth, immortalizing and transforming the protagonists. One may also assume that the memorable deeds thus recounted were reactions to real circumstances (a wild beast, the enemy), not posturing inspired by the protagonists' concern for their future image—that their actions weren't motivated by the desire to be noticed and have their stories told.

In the beginning, fame—positive or negative—was inadvertent, as it often still is. But the resulting popular images, in which the protagonist seemed to exist outside of ordinary life, in a kind of eternity, surely awoke the desire for fame. When Hector, in defense of Troy, challenges the bravest of the besieging Achaeans, he dreams of defeating him and covering himself in glory (*The Iliad*, book VII, trans. A. T. Murray):

And some one shall some day say even of men that
are yet to be, as he saileth in his many-benched ship
over the wine-dark sea: "This is a barrow of a man
that died in olden days, whom on a time in the midst
of his prowess glorious Hector slew." So shall some
man say, and my glory shall never die.

But the thirst for fame also inspired the nobody
who, in 356 B.C., burned down the temple of Arte-
mis at Ephesus (one of the Seven Wonders of the
World) so that his deed would be reported far and
wide. Almost two thousand years later, in the fif-
teenth century, among those close to the sultan of
Turkey, it was "better to be known for something,
even if it wasn't good, than to be known for nothing," according to Fernando de la Torre (María
Rosa Lida de Malkiel, *La idea de la fama en la Edad
Media castellana*). The obsession with self-image is
the subject of Oscar Wilde's novel *The Picture of
Dorian Gray:* "To become a spectator of one's own
life is to escape the suffering of life." "There is only
one thing in the world worse than being talked
about, and that is not being talked about."

Foolish Herostratus managed to make it into
the history books, but he boasted of his crime and
paid for it at the stake (an eye for an eye and a
conflagration for a conflagration). Others came up
with schemes to make themselves famous without
being burned to death. Evidence or intimations of
this plotting circulated in secret, by word of

mouth or letter, in the form of scandalized accusations, gossip intended to sully others' good name, or defensive strategies calculated to turn such cunning ploys to the service of good causes. Marx complained in 1862 about "*La conspiration de silence* with which I am honored by the German mob." Maybe as a result, five years later, he organized a conspiracy so that *Das Kapital* would be acclaimed: "It therefore depends now on the skill and the activity of my Party friends in Germany whether the second volume takes a long or short time to appear...immediate success is the result, not of genuine criticism, but, to put it bluntly, of creating a stir, of beating the drum (December 28, 1862, and October 11, 1867, letters to Kugelmann, trans. Jane Tabrisky).

By the end of the twentieth century, the mindset had changed. Seeking success was no longer considered a shameful passion in lofty milieus. An ambiguous, premonitory moment is captured in a quip by Bernard Shaw, made when Samuel Goldwyn tried to recruit him, along with other big names (he hired Maeterlinck, who had already won the Nobel Prize in literature). Since Shaw wasn't sure whether it was worth his while or not, he is reported to have smoothly said: "The trouble, Mr. Goldwyn, is that you are only interested in art and I am only interested in money" (Alva Johnston, *The Great Goldwyn*). With that, he poked fun

at the airs each of the two put on: the cultural pretensions of a Hollywood producer and the moral
pretensions of a writer in Hollywood.

Sarcastic admissions gave way, finally, to how-
to manuals. Now there are dozens of books on
how to manage your life in order to become
famous. For example: *How to Get Free Press, Self-
Promotion for the Creative Person, Confessions of Shame-
less Self-Promoters, The Unabashed Self-Promoter's
Guide.* These manuals help you launch yourself as
a recognizable market brand, using business and
PR methods. Some give very detailed instructions:
how to sell yourself and be interviewed all over the
country; what to pack in your suitcase; how to
answer questions; how to handle photographs.
Others describe successful marketing campaigns,
or collect advice from people with experience. A
writer tells how she elbowed her way into the
spotlight with a governor who was visiting town
by requesting his autograph for her son. She took
the opportunity to present him with a copy of her
book, and then she made an admiring short speech
about his work—a speech that got him to pause,
got the cameras trained on them, etc.

It's easier to laugh at Marx's pharisaism or
Shaw's sarcasm than at this generous innocence in
sharing know-how. The emphasis now is not on
hidden trickery, but on good tricks and effective
self-management; on the need to overcome shy-

ness and to have faith and never give up, with the assumption that fame is worth every effort. It's this innocent faith that's responsible for the honest disappointment of many whose wishes become reality.

Joey Berlin (*Toxic Fame: Celebrities Speak on Stardom*) collected hundreds of interviews on the realities of fame, and the consensus is notable: There's no such thing as a private life. "That's the one thing I have the greatest regret about, giving up your privacy" (Clint Eastwood). "It's indescribable. I can't imagine people who relish it. It's just not easy to be separated out like that" (Uma Thurman). I've been asked for my autograph while I was sitting on the toilet (Carol Burnett, Tisha Campbell); standing in front of a urinal (Paul Newman, Jason Priestley). You become isolated, even if you don't want to be; not just because you have to be careful, but because even the people you know don't treat you like an ordinary person anymore. "I suffer very much, I really do" (Sophia Loren). They see you as someone you're not, and you hardly know who you are anymore (Jack McDowell, Edward Furlong, Tim Allen, Winona Ryder). I was never a pretty face or a hot body, so where do people get the idea that I'm sexy? (Robert Redford, Sophia Loren, Laura Dern, Pierce Brosnan, Sarah Jessica Parker). It's ridiculous to be named "Sexiest Man in the World"

147

(Sean Connery, Bruce Willis, Mel Gibson, Mark Harmon, Nick Nolte, Paul Newman). It's terrifying, not exciting, when 4,000 women charge you, trying to rip your clothes off (Marlon Wayans). "A sex symbol becomes a thing. I just hate to be a thing" (Marilyn Monroe). The paparazzi terrify me (Emma Thompson, Sally Field, Rob Lowe). "They harass you in your car and drive recklessly" (Lauren Holly). "It's like a bad dream. People have no scruples anymore" (Melanie Griffith). People look for the bad side of everything (Brad Pitt). "Virtue is not photogenic" (Kirk Douglas). "No one ever writes about the clever little twists that I put into songs that I'm so proud of...all they're concerned about is the women in me [sic] life, how much I drink, and how much money I've got" (Rod Stewart). You're honest with them and it's worse (Julia Roberts, Sandra Bullock). "What they say becomes reality. I now have to defend or deny" (Demi Moore). All your acts become public acts. You can't walk outside, go to restaurants or museums. "I've learned to love delivery food" (Luke Perry). I wish I never had to leave home (Sandra Bullock). You become disconnected from reality. My work was inspired by normal life, which I can't live anymore (Quentin Tarantino, Ellen DeGeneres, Will Smith, Robin Williams). It was great when the Beatles played before they were famous. Then it turned into something else.

"Everybody dreams of being rich and famous. Once you get rich and famous you think, 'This isn't it'" (George Harrison). "If I had known about the privacy thing, I might have made a different choice" (Richard Dreyfuss). "Would anybody choose it? No. Anonymity, if you're cool within your own ego and sense of self worth, is a tremendous asset for living a life" (Jack Nicholson).

Actors illustrate the confusion about any celebrity. In their private lives, in the movies, and for the news they embody different characters. But fame blurs the distinctions, and the public image blends private life, roles in celebrated movies, news, gossip, and public relations. Eventually, to be famous is to become an object created by misunderstandings. Not just any object, but an object that attracts many people's attention. A kind of social "miracle" that may bring attention to the miracles of art or that may simply persist as buzz: talking about the talked about.

1. Unsought fame comes when exciting deeds are recreated from memory as verbal objects that the tribe shares. If the protagonist is still living, he may or may not recognize himself in his reflected image and try to modify it or, conversely, make it his own and modify his memory or behavior to fit the image others have of him. The image isn't of his own making, and its author is lost in anonym-

ity. Disconnected from author, protagonist, and the act itself, it is gradually modified as it passes from mouth to mouth, more and more so as time goes by. It replaces real life—the shared experience of people facing real challenges—with a life outside of reality.

2. The thirst for fame springs from a false image of ultimate fulfillment. Life as depicted in that strange alternate reality seems eternal, a fascinating freedom, more desirable than real life. There's something strange, but also satisfying, in the splitting of life that allows one to watch oneself from the outside, like a performance, beyond the concerns of the here and now. The wish to see oneself from the viewpoint of others is also a primitive form of seeking self-consciousness: of examining oneself, defining oneself, conceptualizing oneself.

3. How-to lessons in fame teach the creation and control of an image that's attention-getting in a positive way. This may work up to a point, but the process is ultimately impossible to control. The images take on a life of their own. The attention of others is fickle. The economics of the limelight doesn't rely solely on those in the limelight, but on powerful oligopolic forces and, finally, on the fleeting fashions and whims of the public. It's easy to end up a sorcerer's apprentice.

4. Disillusionment is belated lucidity. To desire objecthood is to abdicate as subject. It is to distance oneself from real life and to turn toward life as depicted in images of fulfillment. Even when the determination to achieve fame exists, and a plan of action is in place, there's little awareness that the presumed fulfillment is a debasement. The real implications aren't clear until it's too late. Being famous means being treated as an object.

The subject's resistance to being treated as an object didn't first appear when movie stars became aware of their captivity. It is present in Descartes, who set the *I* as the central focus of philosophy. In the last paragraphs of his *Discourse on Method*, he says frankly that he wants his work to be read and he wants to know what his readers think of it, but he doesn't want to be celebrated as its author, because fame is "inimical to calm, which I value above all things," so "I will be grateful if I am allowed to live freely."

Descartes was not modest about his great writings. He wanted to share them as a gift from heaven to all. He made a pilgrimage to the shrine at Loreto, to thank the Virgin Mary for them. He didn't think of himself as the source of the miracle, worthy of pilgrimages. He didn't like the confusion. Note that the argument he makes isn't moral (the quest for fame is unworthy of those with higher spiritual values), but purely practical (it's not worth the cost).

The secrets of fame are the trade of public relations, methods for attracting public attention. The true secret lies in the creation and appreciation of glorious words, painting, and music. These are the miracles no one can explain or teach, miracles forgotten.

We may or may not believe that heaven is the real author of miracles (in literature, art, nature, and human acts) or that fame is a burden. But we can't ignore the testimony of so many. This points to an age-old confusion: glory shines in the work and fame goes its own way. Glory remains a mystery. Nobody knows how to make its happiness happen. The birth of fame is a mystery, too, but once stirring it may be manipulated to promote works or names. This might foster the appreciation of great works, or it might simply drum up publicity for big names.

CHAPTER 16

What to Do
with the Mediocrities?

IT PRESENTED ITSELF to me brazenly, and unsettled me. I was alone. No one would ever have to know. But I did my best not to see it, as if it were a blaring commercial thrusting itself upon me. Maybe it had been there before, just outside my field of vision, and I'd refused to see it then, too. It was a foolish, indecent question that wouldn't go away, that demanded attention: What to do with the mediocrities? Why do so many teachers, juries, editors feel like executioners when they reject them? Pressure is let off in secret rants, gossip, jokes, but that's as far as it goes. Why is it so awkward to analyze the problem? What's so offensive about it?

To be average used to be neutral, then it was positive, then negative, and now it's taboo.

In Greek, Latin, and the Germanic languages, the Indo-European root *medhyo* corresponds to neutral terms for something in the middle (in space, in a sequence, in terms of measurement). In English, *intermediate, mean, median, mediate, medieval, medium,* and *middle* are all derived from the same root. In Latin, *mediocris* described a position of middling height, on a mountain or raised ground. The Indo-European root of *ocris* is *ak:* summit, peak. The definition was expanded to include any non-extreme position: *mediocre malum* (Cicero, a mild illness), *mediocris animus* (Cicero, moderate temper), *mediocris vir* (Justin, man of the middle classes). (Calvert Watkins, *The American Heritage Dictionary of Indo-European Roots;* Agustín Blánquez Fraile, *Diccionario latino-español, español-latino.*)

The ancients distrusted lack of restraint, disproportion, excess. This distrust eventually became praise of the happy medium and moderation. Aristotle defines virtue as the middle ground between two extremes (*Nicomachean Ethics,* book II). Horace celebrates the golden mean (*Odes* II). Seneca exalts the disdain for grandeur: "It shows greatness of spirit to scorn large things and to prefer the ordinary to the excessive" (*Letters to Lucilius,* XXXIX). At the beginning of the seventeenth century, Montaigne is still quoting him nearly word for word: Greatness "shows its stature in preferring ordinary things to lofty things" (*Essays,* book III, chap. 13). Around the same time, Hobbes writes that it is generally agreed that "Virtue consisteth in Mediocrity and Vice in Extremes" (*Oxford English Dictionary*).

Contempt for moderation is a new development, only a few centuries old. It seems to appear with the Baroque and its love of excess, grows with the Enlightenment and absolutism, works itself into a frenzy with Romanticism and its cult of the brilliant and the sublime, and turns scientific with eugenics. Nietzsche proclaims the ethic of the superman and rejects Christian compassion as a negation of life: "The weak and the botched shall perish: first principle of *our* charity" (*The Anti-Christ*, number 2, trans. H. L. Mencken).

The twentieth century didn't invent—but did industrialize—military attacks on civilian populations (to sap the morale of enemy forces) and the genocide of undesirables at home (to purify and improve society). All of this monstrousness brought about a heightening of moral conscience. War, for the first time in history, lost prestige. The regulation of human rights abuses weakened state sovereignty. Contempt for lesser cultures became unacceptable—so unacceptable that now no one can be considered inferior. This unrestricted broadening of the taboo subverts the good intentions behind it, because it ascribes value to the negation of all value criteria.

Mediocrity as a taboo subject derives from this relativism. If nothing is inferior, nothing can be

155

rejected. Americanized progress reinforced the taboo. The Third Reich and the Soviet Union crumbled before the U.S. empire, and their myths vanished with them. The Nazi superman and the socialist new man were defeated, replaced by the fanfare for the common man. If every common man is a potential leader, there can be no mediocrities: only stages along the path to personal realization.

There is a paradox in the culture of progress. Greater excellence in all disciplines is sought, as is greater equality among all people. But how to reconcile equality and excellence? Excellence creates inequalities. "If everything in the world were glorious, nothing would be" (Diderot, *Rameau's Nephew*).

Myth overcomes contradictions by hiding them (Lévi-Strauss, *Structural Anthropology*). The myth of progress is a good example: the contradiction it embodies (excellence for all) is obscured by hopes of times getting better. One must simply believe that the quest for excellence is only a temporary source of inequality. Today's contradiction will be resolved tomorrow. Those at the top are not a privileged minority but the promise of excellence within everyone's reach. The advances of progress will reconcile equality and excellence. Everyone will be glorious in an egalitarian tomorrow, to be postponed time and time again. Today's privileges are everyone's future. And they always will be, as a Brazilian humorist might add. ("Brazil is the country of the future, and it always will be!")

The romantic idea that one must aspire to greatness, that the opposite extreme (complete failure) is preferable to mediocrity, breaks with the ancient notion of the balanced life and culminates in the superman who exterminates mediocrities. Since this is repugnant, and since we can't go back to the ancient idea that mediocrity is desirable, we have to pretend it doesn't exist. We have to believe that mediocrity is a stage: all obstacles will be overcome. Or, more radically, that what seems like mediocrity (according to certain criteria) is actually excellence (according to different criteria).

It would be wiser to acknowledge that we're all mediocre in almost every way, and that it doesn't matter; that to strive for greatness in everything is ridiculous. The exception can't be the general rule, and such a rule shouldn't be confused with the true general rule: that each person is unique, because his genetic code, history, conscience, abilities, and tastes together make up a unique being. No two people are alike. In order for one person to be compared to another, he must be reduced to what he isn't: weight, height, age, time in the 100-meter dash, words typed per minute, education, salary, prizes, quality of his translations of Catullus, of his performance of Berio's *Sequenza XI*.

If people are reduced to a single dimension for the purposes of comparison, the norm is average performance, as it is in any statistical distribution; it's ridiculous to want everyone to compete in the 400-meter freestyle at the Olympics and win. It's impossible for everyone to take first place, and it isn't even desirable for them to try. It *is* desirable for everybody to learn how to swim, for enjoyment's sake (and so that they have a useful skill if they fall into the water).

To reduce all people to a single dimension is to demean them. All of society is demeaned if everything is reduced to measuring and being measured. Learning isn't the same as getting good grades; the important thing is to learn. Having fun and suffering, doing battle with the materials, tools, ideas, and circumstances that might be turned to happy solutions, isn't the same as racking up résumé credits or accumulating prestige, positions, money.

As real life gives way to abstraction, one-dimensional measurements are valued more than people and things. At the same time, there's a slide from reality into narcissism. Well-intentioned parents tell their children (to show that they aren't forcing them to follow in their footsteps): "You can be anything you want, even a street sweeper, so long as you're the best street sweeper there is"—which is to push them to narrow their sights, to make less of themselves, not more. Being the number one sweeper (or whatever) is centered on the *I* and the competition, not on effective and satisfying engagement with reality.

This explains the ontological need to qualify, and the pressure on teachers, juries, and editors. When the important thing isn't to learn, to understand, to create, to research, to have fun, to solve problems, or to help, but to compete and win, every test is a Final Judgment that either gets you into heaven, lands you in hell, or consigns you to limbo. That's why there are endless schemes for success as the single goal in life. To deal effectively with reality is to be reduced to dealing in abstractions: measuring and being measured, beating the competition, meeting goals. Sweeping well, swimming with enjoyment, building well-made things, growing as a person, finding creative solutions to the enigmas and problems that reality sets us: all of these take second place to the climber's winning-is-all mentality.

Paradoxically, the pressure to climb culminates in the ascent of mediocrities to power and fame. It is supposed that fiercely competitive Darwinism will enthrone the excellent, not the incompetent. But these races to the top involve plenty of supposedly objective tests whose results aren't as easily measured as swimming times in an Olympic-size pool. It's impossible to be exact when considering a person for a job or a prize, or evaluating the significance of a work. Even the most honest and capable juries may reach different conclusions. If, to avoid discussion, everything is limited to mechanical measurements, the results are absurd. The candidate with the most points may be a mediocrity. The product that sells best may be mediocre. Whatever ranks highest on surveys may be mediocre. The program with the top ratings may be junk.

The race to the top doesn't always favor people with the special skills for the case, but rather those who are best at competing, adapting, handling PR, molding themselves into desirable commodities, passing exams, racking up points, derailing the competition, winning over or pressuring juries, grabbing the microphone and the spotlight, making themselves popular, setting the ball rolling so that no one can stop it. Natural selection on the race to the top favors the emergence of a new Darwinian species: the *Mediocris habilis*.

Someone with the ability to adapt and clamber his way to the top may also possess genuine skills, but he doesn't need them. All he needs to know is how to climb. An even more skilled person may be left behind in the race if he hasn't mastered the arts of the *Mediocris habilis*. This is how we end up in circumstances in which a perfect incompetent becomes number one.

Unfortunately, those who have no interest in what they're doing, and are only interested in credentials, push until they get what they want. Years later, when they achieve power and glory, they become the models for a society reduced to climbing, and the debasement spreads from above. Many lament it, without seeing that it all starts at the bottom, when teachers, juries, and editors become complicit in shoddy work so as not to feel like executioners. And then some poor soul, given the stamp of approval out of pity, exhaustion, or irresponsibility, becomes their boss, their judge, their executioner.

CHAPTER 17

The Glorification
of the Author

THE MYTH OF THE MAN who becomes God is present in religious, political, and artistic life. In art, this ideal takes three forms:

1. A creator of works worthy of admiration, like God
2. An all-seeing (all-loving, all-judging, all-dreaming) consciousness, like God
3. An object of universal worship, like God

The first is the exclusive domain of the artist. The second also stirs mystics, philosophers, lovers. The third inspires the big names in politics, finance, religion, sports, show business.

1. To focus on the work, to master the trade, to wait for inspiration, to bring the work safely to port, like the sailor who knows which way the wind is blowing, seems a modest endeavor. When

Huidobro says, "Poets are little Gods" and "Why do you sing of the rose, oh poets? Make it bloom in your poem!", his creative impulse sounds almost small, artisanal. But he has the ambition of the potter who glimpses the Divine Potter in himself, the only difference a small breath of life-giving air. His is the supreme ambition of the artist who shouts at his sculpture: Speak!

Even the apprentice who sits down to write a sonnet is doing just what Petrarch, Shakespeare, Sor Juana, or Mallarmé did. His technical skills may actually be better, and they should be: because the collection of good sonnets accumulated over the course of history has made us more discerning and demanding. More elusive is the miracle, which both depends and doesn't depend on the poet: the breath of life that turns a little heap of words into a revelation.

There's nothing modest about striving for this, which is the only thing worthy of the true poet. It's a kind of apotheosis, not of the author, but of the work.

2. The glory of the author as absolute subject hails back to the mystical tradition. St. Thomas Aquinas sees God and loses all interest in his work: "It's straw." St. John of the Cross says calmly: "One single thought of man is of greater worth than the whole world." Rimbaud gives up writing. Another young poet who stops writing justifies it this way: "I'm not writing poetry anymore, I'm living it." He meant that he was in love.

The apotheosis of the author as a mind in ecstasy renders unnecessary any objective, visible apotheosis—the revelation manifested in a work, the exaltation of the artist as object of public attention. It is a liberation from accomplishment and career, the transformation of failure into absolute freedom. It's a way of becoming God without works or witnesses, through love, wisdom, the pride of unrealized or misunderstood genius, in the subjective paradises that Timothy Leary preached: turn on, tune in, drop out.

3. The glorification of the author as object of universal applause is reminiscent of the Roman triumphs and ovations for deified heroes and emperors, ceremonies reflected today in the victory lap that bullfighters take around the ring. With the appearance of illustrated newspapers, film, and television, the triumphal parade route was replaced by spaces of visual representation as the sacred place for the subject's ritual transformation into the object of the deifying masses.

Even when the ovation is the friendly salute of a smaller group, a certain distance is established between the active subjects who applaud and the passive, immobilized subject who is applauded and thereby turned into an object. Even in instances of private admiration, there is a kind of contemplation of the other as a subject momentarily turned object, remote and removed.

> What you are
> distracts me from what you say

declares the entranced lover in a poem by Pedro Salinas, by way of excuse. It's a compliment, but also an elegant justification for the *I* who ignores the *you*, the *I* who doesn't listen.

Ordinary person-to-person dealings are easily reestablished after small, friendly ovations and expressions of private admiration. The interruption creates a pedestal, a distance, a spotlight, another world, a sacred space for human sacrifice, that incapacitates the person and deifies him. But it's still possible to return to cordial, natural conversation, refreshed and even vitalized by the epiphany.

And yet it may happen that normality is not restored: that the person carried away by the ovation is lost to himself and remains there on the pedestal, stuck, frozen; that the others are content to leave him there. The definitive interruption of simple person-to-person communication means a loss of freedom on both sides, each defined by its role in the theater of apotheosis and reduced to playing that role.

Mass ovations give rise much more easily to this, although mutual physical presence leaves a tiny opening for freedom even so. But loss is inevitable when the presence offered to the masses is only an image. The capturing and reproduction of an image in the newspaper, in film, and on television has something voodoo-like about it.

How to restore person-to-person interaction in a crowd? It isn't easy. Either the crowd is broken into groups small enough to allow for personal contact (and then it isn't a crowd) or an impersonal relationship is established. The myth of Babel demonizes fragmentation. But a counter-myth overrides it: the communion of all people in a crowd where many different languages are spoken but all are understood, as described in the Acts of the Apostles (2:6).

Impersonal apotheosis can be totalitarian (everyone identifying with the mystical body of the Leader or the Celebrity, which becomes an object of universal veneration) or democratic (everyone achieving glory by becoming God for fifteen minutes, as Andy Warhol suggested).

The myth of salvation through success, as well as the myth of success as corruption, from which one must distance oneself, have given the creative life a confusing twist. What matters isn't the poem, but to appear on television as a poet: to be the object of cameras, ceremonies, and their vampiric thirst for immortality. What matters isn't the poem; it's the ecstasy of the *I*. But the construction of oneself as an object of public attention or a free spirit on the margins of public life isn't the same as the objective construction of a work, and the luck of trapping a passing miracle.

That's another myth, but one worthier of the poet.

CHAPTER 18

From the Microtext to the *I*

AN ORIGINAL TEXT can be composed of just a few words. There are no minimum lengths for creation. Some poems are just a few syllables long (Ungaretti: "M'illumino d'immenso"); some stories are just a few words long (Monterroso: "When he woke up, the dinosaur was still there"). One could even argue that there are whole conceptual fabrics (texts) woven from a single word, like ecology (Haeckel, 1869), eugenics (Galton, 1883), genocide (Lemkin, 1944), cybernetics (Wiener, 1948).

The combination of two or three words can be more creative than many complete works. When Descartes for the first time in history (*Discourse on Method*, part III, 1637) made reference to a provisional morality, he created an unprecedented concept of morality by the simple act of using an adjective in a novel way. He replaced the commandments (divine, social, traditional) with elective values, rules that a person chooses to follow.

To get to this point required years of critical thought, but the creation of the phrase *morale par provision* was surely instantaneous. The words simply came out that way, in unexpected juxtaposition; and as they flowed from his pen or passed through his head, he saw that they were good.

Words themselves have exploratory powers. They seek each other out, find each other, have the ability to be happy together. Does this begin at the molecular level, with the syllables that make up words, and before that, the phonemes that make up syllables? In this elemental state, where there is no text or personal creation, there's still (linguistic) creation. Not all possible combinations of phonemes make syllables, nor do all possible combinations of syllables make words. Why do some work and others not? Maybe linguists, like chemists, will discover the secret of bonds between phonemes: which ones tend to form stable combinations, which don't, and in what order; also, the secret of syllables that make up words, with the added complication of etymological and grammatical derivation (over and above purely prosodic demands) and the simplifications imposed by verbal economy. It goes without saying that at the next level (words combined into phrases) everything becomes even more complicated, because the production of meaning is involved.

1. Origins of the text

No one knows how or when the first texts were created. To string words together when speaking is normal and creative, even if the sentences created only respond to the demands of the moment, and are completely ephemeral. But sometimes a combination so notable is produced that it seizes the attention of those talking, distracting them from the matter at hand and making them focus on the words themselves. And it may happen that this felicitous expression is stamped on the memory, a memorable text that begins to travel from mouth to mouth. A pleasing phrase can spring into being of its own accord. But the listener who recognizes its felicity and takes note of the spontaneously forged sequence in order to repeat the experience, creates the text.

There's an extensive microtextual literature that's little studied as literature because it's still mostly oral, anonymous, and brief. What to do with sayings? Are they a lexical or a literary creation? Are they part of folklore or literature? Can their history be traced, can they be literarily analyzed? History concentrates on works by well-known authors, not on anonymous and oral microtexts. Also, scale is an unusual standard for classification in literary studies, although it's actually the determining factor in the physiognomy of some works, as is obvious in extreme cases: the epigram vs. the long poem, the short short story vs. the *roman fleuve*. Based on this physiognomy, microtexts seem clearly related among themselves. Are they a genre? Are they variations on known genres? The poem and the short-short story might lead us to think so. But is each Hippocratic aphorism a small-scale medical treatise? Are anecdotes history? Where do riddles and jokes fit in? Curiously, there's an extensive nomenclature for the subgenres of microtext, but the genre itself has no name. It has never been recognized that the brevity of microtexts (which makes them perfect for memorization) gives them certain general characteristics: their compactness reduces the structural options, limits the information that can be handled, encourages a tendency to the vivid and neatly turned, requires self-containment (the ability to stand alone), demands memorable qualities (prosodic, semantic, imaginative), and culminates in a graceful form of expression, despite the economy of means. That's where the family air comes from.

Some day someone will study what all of the following have in common: the adage, the advertisement, the anecdote, the cliché, the commonplace, the curse, the dedication, the dictum, the ejaculation, the epigram, the epigraph, the epitaph, the exemplum, the gibe, the *greguería* (invented by Ramón Gómez de la Serna), the haiku, *idées reçues* (recognized, and thus reinvented, by Gustave Flaubert), the jest, the jingle, the joke, the moral, the *mot célèbre*, the motto, the parable, the play on words, the prayer, the proverb, the quip, the quote, the refrain, the rhyme, the riddle, the saying, the short-short story, the slogan. The list could even be longer. Limiting oneself to intellectual microtexts, there are also aphorisms, apothegms, axioms, concepts, definitions, formulas, maxims, notions, philosophemes, postulates, precepts, principles, propositions, rules, subtleties, thoughts, witticisms.

Incidentally, the study of this literature might have practical applications for those learning to write. Brevity is difficult in ways that make it useful as a tool for learning, and easy in ways that are also useful: unlike a novel, the microtext can be taken in at a glance, seen from every point of view, written a thousand times over. Classes on the art of writing memorable phrases would be a useful introduction to classes in poetry-writing, short story-writing, novel-writing, and playwriting.

2. Origins of the author

It's important to distinguish between impersonal creation, anonymous texts, and an author's oeuvre.

It would be simple enough to build a singing machine, powered by the wind in a garden and programmed with a random succession of every possible syllable (spoken in a beautiful voice, perhaps with harp accompaniment, in the Greek fashion). The wild succession of syllables would sometimes produce miracles, meanings uttered by chance, and even new words never spoken before. These texts would be impersonal works, creations for the listener capable of marveling at them, of recognizing miracles.

Similarly, there are the so-called creative typographical errors that improve a sentence or phrase. No one can take credit for them, but they acquire authorship when the author notices them and makes them his own; when he sees that they're good. The same thing can happen with a slip of the tongue, or the hand, a frequent occurrence in the creative process. There's some innate force of invention in the way words appear of their own accord. The very notion of a slip of the tongue or a slip of the pen acknowledges the act of involuntary creation: speaking and writing before it's clear what's being said. (Those who mock inspiration are overlooking this fundamental reality in order to concern themselves with something secondary: criticizing the lazy.) It even happens in the literature of ideas, in which a creative mistake changes not just words but the course of thought. It's easy to guess in some texts that the author was thinking of something else, about to say something else, and that in the process, because of a slip in forming a phrase, he discovered an unexpected thought.

Personal creation can consist of recognizing a chance sequence of words as one's own and correcting it or not: a sequence formed by a singing machine, a creative slip, or the magnetic force of the words themselves. There may be a deliberate attempt to produce felicitous combinations. The stamp of the creator may be evident. And yet, personal creation can still be anonymous. This is common in the oral tradition, in which more attention is paid to the felicity of a phrase than to the name of the author. A saying, a riddle, implies a creator, even if the work is unattributed, its author forgotten, and its words gradually altered as it passes from mouth to mouth. In the case of the Homeric poems and other great works, it would be ridiculous to suppose that they were produced by accident. There was a conscious process of creation.

Anonymous texts aren't impersonal creations. Nor are they the work of a collective author (the people). They're the result of society's and the creator's ignorance of intellectual property, or lack of concern for it. Attribution, the control of reproduction and revision, and the collection of royalties are later developments. Authorship is born with the first of these rights (the identification and recognition of the author), but goes further. The presence of the author in the text is strengthened:

by some reference of the author to himself; by the hallmark of his style, distinct from that of other authors; by his subject matter and approach, traditional or not; by the creation of textual forms that are a reflection of the author, whether implicitly (his way of seeing, a wink of complicity directed at the reader) or explicitly (Catullus addressing himself to Catullus, St. Augustine examining his conscience); and, ultimately, by the creation of the author as a work, the character implicit or explicit in the text leaping from the page to play a role in public life.

The public figure of the author may be a legend created by his readers, so far removed from the idea he has of himself that he's offended and rejects it. But it may also be a project he undertakes himself, consciously or unconsciously, working (or not) from the legend: the creation of a trademarked public persona, carefully managed and sold. The author can manage his literary name like a brand, with a whole line of products: books published under his name (but not necessarily entirely written by him), with all their subsidiary rights (translations, compilations, adaptations, films, videos, albums); as well as a line of services: readings, lectures, appearances at ceremonies, board membership, consulting, endorsements, blurbs, the bestowing of prizes, interviews. He can even make the move to industrial design. There's no reason that toys, clothes, and many other things should be the sole province of characters like Harry Potter and Mickey Mouse. At the Günter Grass Museum, established with the participation of the writer, Günter Grass t-shirts or Günter Grass tin drums could surely be sold.

To see only the commercial in this, to criticize the industry of fame, is once again to concern oneself with something of secondary importance and to forget the fundamental point: to create a text is to create the creative personality, establishing it objectively as a creative subject. The character of the author is always present in the text, implicitly or explicitly, discreetly or overwhelmingly. His protagonism can be healthy or pathological, commercial or not. There are also those whose prominent roles in politics, religion, and social life are scripted: monologues, theatricality.

3. Extreme genres

There are two literary genres that seem to precede and follow all others: the microtext and the literature of the *I*. The microtext hails from prehistoric times, and is the universal proto-genre. The literature of the *I* is a later development, and has the feel of a universal post-genre: it follows in the wake of established genres, whose end it seems to proclaim.

A history of this evolution is needed. There are stirrings of such a project in Hegel's *Aesthetics* (last chapter). As Hegel writes, the epic poetry of the *Iliad*, the *Odyssey*, the *Ramayana*, is objective, innocent of its own *I*. Its subjective antithesis is lyric poetry, which speaks from the *I*. Synthesis comes with dramatic poetry, which (in a kind of higher objectivity) presents the dialogue of subjects who speak from the *I*. Once this culmination is reached (the consciousness of the self, the consciousness of the consciousness of others), the supreme function of art and religion (the expression of the absolute) becomes unnecessary, because intellectual consciousness is enough; what follows is reflection, humor, the search for subjective and contingent interests, the dissolution of art. "On the side of its highest destiny, art is a thing of the past" (Introduction). All that remains is engagement with works that already exist and the creation of parodies, intertexts, interventions, conceptual proposals, radical breaks, and theories of art, instead of art.

Despite Hegel's pessimism, it may be observed that this evolution seems to take place without the extinction of species:

a. Oral literature hasn't disappeared. On the contrary, it has prospered with the telephone and sound recordings. It coexists with written literature and the new oral literatures of the radio and television.

b. The microtext hasn't disappeared. On the contrary, in written literature the fragment has become a paradigm of modernity. Paradoxically, it flourishes at the same time as the *roman fleuve,* novel cycles, and the industry of complete works.

c. Anonymous literature hasn't disappeared. On the contrary, it has blossomed and grown on the internet. Social criticism, jokes, plays on words, and tall tales (hospital stories, taxi stories, car and plane trip stories) circulate by word of mouth or from computer to computer.

Furthermore, the prominence of the subject who creates himself as an object (commercial or not) coexists with the philosophical negation of the subject (Foucault). It coexists with the emphasis on the work as an object independent of the creative subject, whose catalyzing presence leaves no personal traces (Eliot); with the dream of writing lyrics so popular that the name of the author is forgotten (Machado); with the search for an automatic writing (Breton); the project of writing by juxtaposing quotes from other authors (Benjamin); the game of writing with restrictions or mechanical formulas (Oulipo). It coexists with authors who shy away from biographers, interviewers, and photographers (Traven, Salinger, Blanchot).

The end of poetry, which Plato desired and Hegel announced as historical fact is echoed in other desires, lamentations, or premature announcements: the end of the novel, genres, tonal music, easel painting, religion, ideologies, metaphysics, man, history. It even seems plausible in the face of the excessive production of dull, mediocre works (and impressive résumés). But the myth of the end (apocalyptic or not) is an age-old story, refuted by its own continuity. Creative droughts (which sometimes last centuries), the debasement of culture, vacuousness: these are undeniable but intermittent historical realities. They aren't the disaster of the end of all times, but the discouragement that accompanies the passing of all times. Horace thought (*Ars Poetica*) that the Romans were no longer capable of writing like the Greeks, because from the time they were children they had learned to crave lucre rather than literary glory. He overlooked the fact that, ten years before, enthused by his own *Odes* (III), he had declared them immortal. He overlooked the fact that the next generation (Tibullus, Propertius, Ovid) would emulate his enthusiasm, not his pessimism.

The declared theoretical impossibility of producing a great poem, a great novel, a great painting, evaporates each time an artist does in practice what theoretically can no longer be done. His achievement may be an exception, but the argument still holds, because the great works of the past were also exceptional cases amid mediocrities now forgotten. It's absurd to become discouraged because mediocrity is the norm — today as always. We don't judge the past by its legions of mediocrities, but by its miracles.

It's from this perspective that one should view the appearance of works that mix and blur conventional genres. The practice is usually interpreted as an exercise of freedom that signals the end of genre distinctions, but it's really the extreme form of an ancient phenomenon: the thematized presence of the *I* writing about the *I* writing, in Catullus, Horace, St. Augustine, Montaigne, Cervantes, Pirandello; in epistolary and autobiographical literature; in self-portraits, in Velazquez's *I* painting himself painting, in Escher's hands drawing themselves; in the epistolary qualities of Haydn's *Farewell Symphony;* in the authorial irony of Satie.

All the arts can shift from interest in the work to interest in the author. Every genre can shift toward the *I* as post-genre. Any bundle of heterogeneous materials can be co-opted and unified by the theme of the *I*, in the same way that the author of a letter, autobiography, or diary, can insert pages by himself or by others, from very different genres, introduced (or not) by an explication such as, "Then I wrote this poem," "In the news today," "Foolproof spider repellant." What appears to be a hybrid is in fact hubris, the hubris of the *I* as genre. The urge to explore it and the opportunities it presents have caused it to flourish. It has reached its zenith with the emergence of the blog.

Creating oneself as an object of interest is now so popular that it's becoming a new kind of anonymity. We are not at the end of art, or the end of genres. We are in the midst of a boom of the *I* as literature, an old art whose appeal (exhibitionism) is also its limitation. More often than not, the *I* is boring.

Literature existed before the *I*. The first texts were created before the emergence of writers. The first instance of creative consciousness may be attributed to the listener who hears a memorable phrase and recognizes the marvel produced by the randomness of talk. Reading, not writing, is in the origin of literature. It is texts and literature that develop consciousness, through the reading of what's written by chance, by others or by oneself. Consciousness is created by works, not the other way around.

The author arises from the work, possessing the luck to spot a passing miracle and the craft to trap it. He doesn't step into the trap of fame, which is a different matter entirely. A greater awareness of the authorial *I*, and even an exhibitionistic streak, may aid in the creation of great work, as Catullus and St. Augustine demonstrate; but the important outcome is the masterpiece itself. The secret of its glory remains a mystery, even for the author. Nobody knows where masterpieces come from. Miracles are miracles. They catch us before we catch them. But we're not trapped by them — we're set free.